# INTUITION
## The Voice of God

# DEBBIE N. GOLDBERG

Copyright ©2022 by Debbie N. Goldberg
INTUITION
The Voice of God
by Debbie N. Goldberg

Printed in the United States of America

For information from the publisher, address at Debbie N. Goldberg
deb.goldberg@verizon.net

ISBN # 978-0-9983227-8-0 – Paperback Book
ISBN # 978-0-9983227-7-3 - E-Book
ISBN # 978-0-9983227-3-5 - Audio Book

All rights reserved solely by the author. The author guarantees all contents are original and do not infringe upon the legal rights of any other person or work. No part of this book may be reproduced in any means, graphic, electronic, or medical, including photocopying, recording, taping or by any information storage retrieval system without the permission of the authors except in the case of brief quotations embodied in critical articles and reviews.

Because of the dynamic nature of the internet, any web addresses or links contained in this book may have changed since publication and may no longer be valid. The views expressed in this work are solely those of the author.

The author of this book does not dispense medical advice or prescribe the use of any technique as a form of treatment for physical, emotional, medical, or Spiritual problems without the advice of a physician, either directly or indirectly. The only intent of the author is to offer information of a general nature to help you in your quest for emotional and Spiritual well-being.

Cover Design – Debbie N. Goldberg
Interior Design – DTPerfect Book Design

*Intuition is a deep connection
to your Knowingness.
It is Divine Wisdom.*

The original text was internally dictated to me by Archangel Michael in 2016. Over the last six years I have had to grow into and integrate the wisdom that was given to me. I have combined these new insights with the original text resulting in this updated co-creation. I am so very grateful to Michael for his gift that enables me to present this new book to you.

It is my deepest desire for you to awaken and find the Love within yourself that you have been searching for. There is no other experience that can compare to that of being in union with your Creator. The word bliss is neither deep enough nor expansive enough to describe the joy and healing that comes from God's unconditional Love. You must experience it for yourself. Dive deep within and find everything that you have been looking for.

*This book is dedicated to my husband, my children and their families, their children, and the ones yet to come… I hold you all in such high esteem, Love, and Light for you have been my greatest teachers. As God's Love and Wisdom heals me from generations of family pain, societal programing, and my own experiences it automatically sets you up to heal as well. For if I have done my job of healing myself and come into who I truly Am then I have paved the way for you and contributed to your own spiritual path of love, healing, and purpose. There is no greater gift that a parent can give their child or to the collective human family. It is a gift of Love to you from the bottom of my heart. These books are my legacy of Love to all of you. Remember to always listen for the Voice of Love within.*

# Contents

**Chapter 1:** Intuition is Divine Knowingness. . . . . . . . . . . . 1

**Chapter 2:** What is Consciousness?. . . . . . . . . . . . . . . . 7

**Chapter 3:** Reviving Your Intuition . . . . . . . . . . . . . . . 25

**Chapter 4:** The Natural State of Being is Love. . . . . . . . . 63

**Chapter 5:** Your Intuition is Always Accessible . . . . . . . . 91

**Chapter 6:** The Rebellion of the Ego. . . . . . . . . . . . . . . 103

**Chapter 7:** Examples of Resistance . . . . . . . . . . . . . . . 123

**Chapter 8:** Taming the Will and Learning Self-Discipline . 143

**Chapter 9:** Destination Intuition. . . . . . . . . . . . . . . . . 161

**Chapter 10:** Why Do We Resist Taking Time For What We Need?. . . . . . . . . . . . . . . . . . . 169

**Chapter 11:** Procrastination and Commitment . . . . . . . . . 181

**Chapter 12:** Your Responsibility to You. . . . . . . . . . . . . 195

**Chapter 13:** Believing in Your Self . . . . . . . . . . . . . . . . 221

**Chapter 14:** Being Purposely Intuitive . . . . . . . . . . . . . 245

**Chapter 15:** Happiness it Shall Be . . . . . . . . . . . . . . . . 253

**About the Author**. . . . . . . . . . . . . . . . . . . . . . . . . . 263

**Acknowledgments**. . . . . . . . . . . . . . . . . . . . . . . . . 267

## Chapter One

### INTUITION IS DIVINE KNOWINGNESS

*God, please help me remember
our Divine Union and sustain
this Knowingness in me
through every moment.
Amen*

We are blessed in miraculous ways on this earth. We do not understand the depth of this blessing due to our inability to see or know our inner wisdom while we are in the limited dream state of unconsciousness. We are all embarked on a Supernatural experience (incarnation) where we must awaken from our deep Spiritual slumber. Even when we do awaken, it takes time before we can begin to understand the illusion of life. Only then can we start to integrate all the Wisdom and Knowingness of the Divinity that lies deep within us all. The source of this Wisdom and Knowingness is what I call God. Our intuition is the Voice of God, the Voice of Love, it is our voice.

We rely on our human eyes to see and know. It is not in our human nature to believe things we cannot see or understand. This, amongst other distractions, detaches us from our Divine intuition. From time to time we may get a strong feeling, image, thought, hear a voice, or have a vision about something, but determining whether these arise from our intuition, or our ego programing/false sense of self can be difficult to discern.

Sometimes we listen to our intuition and other times we do not. We don't want to ignore what our eyes see, but we want our intuition to be our guide of Truth. Trusting our intuition takes time and practice. It is an enormously important part of the journey to learn how to rely on our Divine Knowingness and not our ego, physical senses, or earthly programing.

This book is about tuning-in to our intuition (Divine Knowingness) all the time so that it supersedes what our eyes see, what our senses tell us and what we think we already understand. Our Divine Knowingness is Divine Revelation, and it is the source of Truth, Wisdom and Knowledge about our Self and the world at large. We will only find the power to disregard the ego's faulty beliefs by learning to trust our intuition.

## INTUITION IS DIVINE KNOWINGNESS

*Our belief that we need to be changed, healed or be something other than what we are is a misconception. God does not heal us. He re-parents us with unconditional Love and Divine wisdom so that we can see that we are already perfect and whole: we were never broken. This understanding heals and restores us. He teaches us to perceive our traumatic experiences in a different Light, the Light of Divine understanding.*

During a difficult time in my life, I chose to open my heart to understand myself more. I wanted to know what I was doing that was causing myself so much emotional pain. I learned a meditation practice, called guided imagery. Unknowingly, it opened the door to the voice of Jesus, God, John the Baptist, and the Angels. Not only was I able to hear, but I was able to see symbolic images, have visions and feel the presence of Love itself within my very being. Through this meditative practice I was able to form a beautiful reciprocal relationship with my Spiritual guides. These Divine forms are aspects of my Consciousness, created to guide me throughout my personal journey.

There is only Oneness, One Divine Consciousness, through which God/Love reveals itself in all creative forms to help us through the journey of incarnation. We are creative Consciousness experiencing itself at different levels of awareness.

What I have learned through this awakening process is that I had to connect and build a trusting relationship with my Spiritual guides first before I learned to trust my intuitive instincts. This is still a work in progress. As I evolve, my relationship with God/Self deepens.

I was a willing participant in wanting to have an intimate relationship with God. This openness to experience what was within, flooded me with unconditional Love, Divine wisdom, deep healing, peace, guidance, and gifts. I learned to trust my Spiritual guides for everything. As you are building trust in your guide(s) you then start to build trust within your Self as your belief in Divine Truth grows.

The Divine unfolds and reveals itself in whatever form you personally feel comfortable with. It knows every intimate detail about you because it is you. The form it takes has all to do with the story that was written for and by you. You are the Creator and its creation. As creation you are the eternally protected experiencer of your dream life.

*God is the pure
energy of unconditional Love.*

## INTUITION IS DIVINE KNOWINGNESS

There are only myths to describe your incarnation experience. In this human form there is no way to understand the expansiveness of God/Creation. Even when you awaken you will still not grasp the expansiveness of what you/God is. The only Truth that I Know and have experienced, is that God is Love. Jesus has given me a myth to help me understand my incarnation experience that I am sharing with you.

Upon awakening, I needed an explanation to try to understand my experiences. Over time you start to accept the simple truth that God is good, you are good, He Loves you, and you are just having a playful dream experience… although, I know very well that at times, it does not feel that way. Our ultimate purpose is to enjoy the gift of life and to be happy Knowing that everything is always in Divine order and protection.

## Chapter Two

WHAT IS CONSCIOUSNESS?

*It is a state of mind or of being. It is Love,
Light and Knowledge. It is eternal and
infinite invisible energy that has no form.
It is Divine unconditional Love,
and it is what I am calling God.*
*-Jesus-*

Due to the belief in duality there appears to be two versions of Consciousness. Divine Consciousness is God. Human consciousness, what we perceive through our senses, is an illusion. Human consciousness is permeated by the ego thought system. Divine Consciousness is imagination. It is an expansive intelligence that is infinite and eternal. It is the source of all creation.

As humans, it sometimes helps us to understand things if we can put them into a visual context because we cannot perceive or conceive nothingness. It might be helpful to envision Divine Consciousness as a kind of floating mind, a sea of Love, invisible essence, the expansiveness of the universe, the beauty of creation or the air that you breathe.

*Imagine...the beautiful blue Heavenly sky is always present and unchangeable. It is God, Divine Consciousness. The clouds are thoughts that drift in and out of Consciousness. The clouds change form, and many times hide the fact that the beautiful blue sky even exists. This is our experience. Consciousness is always present; we just drift in and out of it following the movement of our thoughts.*

Nothing else exists except for God Consciousness. There is no gender, religion, race, or form. However, when we connect with the Divine, we tend to visualize that Spiritual energy as coming to us in human or symbolic form. Others will see or relate to Light, Divine beings, nature, or an animal. Some will just hear a voice(s) and others will connect through a profound **'Knowingness'** in their heart, which translates words of Divine wisdom for them. The Divine world or God's Kingdom is only benevolent.

# WHAT IS CONSCIOUSNESS?

*For this physical life experience, Divine Consciousness appears as different forms of creation. Every relationship is a relationship with God/Self for nothing else exists. You can think of yourself as Divine Consciousness because there is only Oneness. You are One 'creating and experiencing your life.'*

We all have the ability to experience our Divine nature in all of these ways, but each person connects in a way that is comfortable for them…a way that is unique to their journey and the Divinely purposeful individual story created just for them.

My experience is being able to see the Divine as human form, hear and understand through Knowingness. I see, Know, and feel God, Jesus, John, Angels, and family who have passed on. This is the individual story that has been created for me to awaken, heal and have purpose in this life.

Although I Know that Divine Consciousness is not separate individuals and has no form or gender, I personally relate to God as male, for that is the way He reveals Himself to me for my journey. Therefore, I use the term He for God. You can replace terms with anything you feel comfortable with since God answers to all names and symbols, for there is no separation there is only Love.

Through these Divinely guided relationships, you are building connection and trust with your *intuition*. You eventually come to realize it is one and the same Knowledge *as Divine Love because it is your True nature and guidance*. Yet, for the incarnation experience you continue to see yourself as separate. Over time, you will integrate more wisdom and believe in your Divine nature.

*Our Spiritual guide and our intuition (our being) are one and the same. You are Spirit. You are Consciousness.*

*Your intuition is the Divine connection with and as your Creator, which means you always have access to the Divine realm, as you are One energy... God Consciousness.*

*There is only One Mind, and it is God.*

Our Divine Knowledge increases as our Consciousness expands. Some people refer to Consciousness as being in the 'now' moment, or aware, but it is much more expansive than that. Consciousness is the realization of the Oneness of all things. It is energy in the form of thought that is creatively taking shape through our senses to enable us to physically experience life. Consciousness is all that exists; there is nothing else. It is Divine Love. It is God's power and creativity.

## WHAT IS CONSCIOUSNESS?

Our journey is remembering and believing that we are Divine. Even though we believe we are growing in Consciousness we are actually returning Home to who we were (and still are) before we invented a self to experience different states of Consciousness. We purposely forgot that we are Divine so we can have these amazing awakening encounters with symbolic Divine forms that prod us into remembering. It is an amazing Divine fantasy! As we grow in our relationship with our Spiritual guide, it increases our Self-awareness. This, in turn, builds self-esteem and self-trust. We can now give our self the grace that is necessary to deconstruct the false self we created and allow our True Self to unfold in Divine timing.

> *Eventually you realize that you are One and the same as Divine Knowledge. You are the same Consciousness. Through the awakening process your new belief system integrates into Oneness. You are God walking and talking in creative form. God is you!*

The Divine reawakening process entails the systematic deconstruction of a false self and its faulty beliefs through an ongoing teaching curriculum that reprograms you to remember your Divinity. As your True Self unfolds you begin to express your inner beauty by allowing your creativity to come to the surface. Together, with Divine guidance, you explore it, refine it, and share it with others, as you are being cultivated/transformed through the Divine relationship. This is why it is so important to establish an intimate relationship with God.

Transformation is what I believe the term born again means. You do this by carving out time to be quiet so you can hear, listen, and have intimate conversation. You hear God's Voice in your own voice. It always meets you where you are in the most loving ways.

Your journey is a process of development, maturing and of polishing you for the role you were created for. There is a Divine plan for your life that is very different than what your false self believes your purpose is. You are unknowingly following a preplanned, individualized Divine curriculum that contains specific lessons, experiences, purposes created just for you. You get glimpses of it over time because your intuitive heart remembers it is here to do something unique…something special. All your transformation is Divinely carried out within you and over time your external experience will reflect this.

God is moving you as you. God is taking care of everything for you. The transformation process is dismantling the false self. This false self was Divinely orchestrated, created by the ego for purposes of forgetfulness and to build an individual story about you for the incarnation journey.

## WHAT IS CONSCIOUSNESS?

What we call incarnation is just a virtual physical experience of life. Each person the star in their own personal movie. The journey is a process by which we explore and re-awaken to more expansive levels of our Divine creative Consciousness. God is always Divinely guiding you through this transformation process to awaken from the dream of being human.

Because of your willingness to participate in this process, you allow God's Will to come through you in peaceful delightful ways. This occurs when we are aware, awake, and conscious of Divine Truth through the relationship with a Divine guide. This is what we call co-creating.

Your will and God's are one and the same, but you forgot due to the trance of the ego. When you allow your talents, Love and Light to shine, it helps others find their own personal inner light (God's Light) healing and creativity. Your ego will try to prevent you from exploring your internal creativity because it believes that you can't provide your own happiness; but this, of course, is false. Happiness and Joy are the core of who you are. It is your Divine nature.

So how do we feel our way into a true connection with our intuition? It certainly isn't a skill that's taught at home or in school…although it should be. I have found that being still, silent, meditating, praying, and asking questions within allows us to witness the beauty of who we are, Love itself.

INTUITION

When we listen to our inner world of Love, we learn how all things come to be through our Creator's unconditional Love and Wisdom. We are taught who we are, a Divine being, Consciousness, and why we are here. You are sung the most beautiful Love song just for you.

We are prodded to constantly remember who we are because it is easy to forget. It is impossible to want to return to our former trance-state again because when present, we understand God as our lifeline. At this moment nothing else matters, nothing else exists. We now Know that we are connected to the Light, Love and One mind of Creation that brings us into complete balance through Divine nature and Its Truth.

You just need to learn what interferes with hearing or trusting your intuition as well as ways to empower your inner Wisdom. You will find the peace and comfort that comes from trusting your Self and tapping into the Wisdom of Divine **Consciousness** that is always supporting you on your journey. You are a miracle; your life is a miracle, and you are and have an amazing story that continues to unfold.

> The journal entries you will be reading are intimate conversations between me, God, Jesus, and other Divine entities. Even though I speak of several Divine entities...

## WHAT IS CONSCIOUSNESS?

because that is the way I experience them...
they represent One Voice which is
Divine Consciousness.

---

Journal Entries 11/17/17 – 11/20/17
Meditation With Jesus

---

I am in meditation with Jesus, and we are facing each other. He puts his index finger up and tells me to look at a point on the tip of his finger. This is what he explains to me:

**Jesus:** There is only one point of existence, and it is Consciousness. That Consciousness is God. There is no separation. Pure Consciousness encompasses all Divine Knowledge. That is why we call it Higher Consciousness. As Consciousness there is nothing more to learn. The role of a human is to remember that you already are pure loving God Consciousness. So, as the veil of unconsciousness keeps lifting, meaning we just had an expansive awareness, we are not actually learning Higher Consciousness, although it feels that way. We are actually REVEALING our own existing level of Consciousness. We are getting to see a part of who we already are.

As pure Consciousness there are no lessons to learn, but as a human and for this human experience there are. The process of awakening and remembering keeps bringing you closer to the essence of what you already are. As a human, the unveiling process brings you to a place of understanding that there is much more to you and this Universe then you could ever understand.

**Me:** At the moment when I am observing myself from within or witnessing all that is going on within me, I am in my Consciousness, but only at the level of my awakening. So, is it true that all of the incarnations are about remembering that we are at some level of Consciousness, but we never stop reincarnating because we'll never be able to attain a complete understanding of pure God Consciousness? Is it true that as long as we are in human form, we can never get there? I am hearing that as humans our ability to understand is finite, while pure God Consciousness is infinite and eternal?

**Jesus:** Yes.

**Me:** What is Consciousness?

## WHAT IS CONSCIOUSNESS?

**Jesus:** It is a state of mind or state of being. You recognize it as being present or in a "now" moment, but it is much more expansive than that. Consciousness is everything.

**Me:** Is Consciousness part of the illusion?

**Jesus:** No, it is not. It is all that exists. There is nothing else. It is Love, Light, and Knowledge. It is God's power and creativity.

**Me:** The word collective implies there is separation.

**Jesus:** Yes, it does. But we use the word for teaching purposes. Once one truly understands the idea of a single Consciousness, it is easy to understand that there is only One Consciousness…. God Consciousness.

**Me:** You said everything and everyone in my illusion is me. My Consciousness creates the world and people I experience?

**Jesus:** Yes, very good.

**Me:** Other people are not God Consciousness?

**Jesus:** They are *your creative illusion*.

**Me:** Help me understand please.

**Jesus:** They are all Consciousness because you cannot separate Consciousness.

**Me:** So, what we are calling a Spirit or Soul is really just Consciousness?

**Jesus:** Yes, that would be a good way to describe it.

**Me:** So, everyone is part of my own consciousness and I am theirs'?

**Jesus:** Yes, because you are all One Consciousness.

**Me:** Everyone is different parts of my Consciousness, but what we see is steeped in an illusion that allows us to experience things?

**Jesus:** Yes. You are seeing parts of your Consciousness played out for learning and experiencing different parts or aspects of you. It is God's will that this is done in order to re-experience your Oneness.

Debbie, because we perceive we exist in both worlds simultaneously, ethereal and earthly, we live in duality. Duality is everything we see and experience. They reside togeth-

## WHAT IS CONSCIOUSNESS?

er just like the sun and the moon, water and fire, air and earth, Truth and ignorance, Light and dark, Highest and ego, mountains and valleys, beauty and unsightly, rich and poor, black and white, peace and hatred, fear and confidence. Darkness is actually ignorance or unconsciousness.

Karma or Soul Print Energy consciousness is part of the illusion of incarnating. It is Divinely orchestrated for this experience. Its purpose is to make the physical experience seem real. As Consciousness there is only perfection.

**Me:** That is quite a large story about the illusion, Jesus.

**Jesus:** The Karma is a way of letting go and understanding the being you truly are through forgiveness and making better choices.

**Me:** So there really are no Karmic cords to cut? What is cutting cords a metaphor for?

**Jesus:** It is part of the story of incarnation. It is a metaphorical understanding that implies you have moved more into the Light and away from ignorance. One would need to want to cut the cord for the right reason which is to truly forgive, let go, and bless versus just severing patterns. Remember this is all part of the incarnation story. You don't want to get lost in all the stories.

# INTUITION

**Me:** I guess I have been writing about the Soul Print energy as an illusion, but it just hit me in a more expanded way. I see more clearly that there is only Love. If I understand this, it should take all the pressure off. All the stories we learned about the illusion of incarnating are not real either. They are part of the Earth story. I just need to keep remembering God is in control of everything because it is difficult to understand.

**Jesus:** Yes. You need to continue to participate in life without fear and worry.

**Me:** Duality does not live in Consciousness?

**Jesus:** No, only in the human experience, and it is perfection.

**Me:** As the Light keeps exposing ignorance, the ignorance (darkness) turns to Light?

**Jesus:** Yes. The ignorance becomes transformed to Light. This is what happens as the veil keeps lifting. The Light, Wisdom, and Knowledge is revealed and expanded. Ignorance is now transmuted or balanced by the Light. Ignorance becomes awareness. This is a difficult concept to describe.

# WHAT IS CONSCIOUSNESS?

During meditation, Jesus drew a diagram, and I copied it into my journal. Jesus called the diagram The Wheel of Faith and Love. He asked that I recreate it on the computer. This is what you see on the next page. It was a lesson for me to understand and integrate within myself. I realize that this diagram is not just for me it is for everyone. Jesus explained how to interpret the diagram.

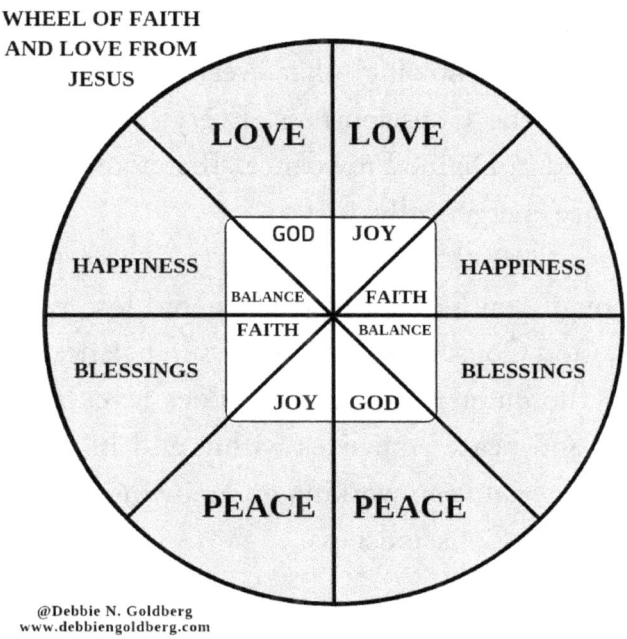

@Debbie N. Goldberg
www.debbiengoldberg.com

# INTUITION

*God's greatest Joy is Loving you.
Believing this brings you Peace.
Having Faith brings your Happiness into
Balance because you understand
You Are Blessed*
*- Jesus -*

**Jesus:** Inside the square is Consciousness. It is God. It is who you, Me, and everyone are. Joy is a Divine state of being. Faith is "Knowing" that everything is in Divine order within the Consciousness. Everything is working perfectly and in Divine Providence. Therefore, everything is in balance energetically.

Even though you feel out of balance and lose your faith at times, God Consciousness is always in balance, it never changes. The outer ring which includes love, happiness, blessings, and peace actualizes within and in your outer experience as you keep working on Knowing that you are One with God Consciousness.

Every time you come to God, or Me, which is going to God, you are being balanced energetically, and it restores your faith in believing that everything is okay.

You keep coming Home to the center, the nucleus of who we truly are. As a human being we need to keep doing this daily. Drink in the Divinity and continue to grow by developing this relationship with God, this relationship with Self actually, since there is no separation.

The Truth is that you are the square of the diagram. You are the center, the Oneness. You keep coming Home to your Self, even though you continue to feel and believe in separation because of the ego. You are coming Home to you. For you are God. There is nothing else. Do you understand, Debbie?

**Me:** I do, and I get glimpses of the Oneness, but not as often as I would like to.

**Jesus:** Your ego is doing a great job as it was made to. It will continue to get easier in time. No pressure. You are exactly where you should be. It's a concept that's hard to explain and difficult to truly integrate. How about you just let this percolate for a while?

**Me:** I guess it is hard to imagine that I am God. I wonder if I called God by a different name such as Consciousness, it might be easier to accept.

**Jesus:** You could do that, but then you are missing the point of Divine Love. The term Consciousness does not bring God's Divine essence into the meaning. If you

## INTUITION

leave God out of it, you lose out on understanding how much you are Love and Loved.

## Chapter Three

REVIVING YOUR INTUITION

*Life is a playground. You are supposed to be having fun and enjoying your life. You are here to Spiritually re-awaken, to consciously expand, mature and to remember who you are.*

Have you ever felt that you knew something was going to happen before it actually did happen? Or maybe you knew to do or not to do something, yet you did the exact opposite anyway? Some people will use the terms crown chakra, third eye, mind's eye, inner eye, pineal gland, sixth sense, or Divine/high heart to describe a connection to Divine Consciousness, but it is all the same guidance intuited in different ways.

# INTUITION

*Our intuition is an invitation to an intimate relationship with God...to go deeper within, explore and expand our self-awareness as Love itself.*

We tend to disregard our intuition because, as children, we weren't encouraged or taught how to tune-in to our natural instinct in order to develop it. Instead, we were programed to listen to authority, society and our physical five senses.

As a result, the ego, the false and immature sense of self takes over as our lives progress. We become governed by our fears and to what the ego tells us we need to do to remain safe, to be loved, to be happy and to avoid pain. So why have we not been listening to our Divine intuition?

The ego sets the stage for how we experience life by creating all the contrasting thoughts and perceptions (good and bad, right, and wrong, safe, and fearful, Divine, and evil, etc.) that create conflict and shift our mind away from who we truly are and what this life is… pure Divine fun, innocence, and joy. It creates all the stories and dramas that we experience in our lives. It is like a movie projector propelling all our stories onto the illusionary Earth stage. Yet, it also provides opportunities for us to choose what we want to believe through contrasting thoughts.

The ego can be thought of as a catalyst for this life experience. It helps create the illusion that we are an individual, a physical entity, a human being. The ego is an energetically shared collective experience. There is only one ego because there is only One mind of Consciousness. We share everything although there is only One. The ego thought system is Divinely orchestrated for us to have a 'life experience.'

Even though we live in the ego's illusion our intuition tells us that that there is something more than meets the eye. It keeps prodding us to awaken from the illusion and to keep searching for the Truth.

The ego voice or thought system is an illusion in itself because **the ego is a false sense of self**, it is not real. Nevertheless, it feels very real, and we believe it to be our own voice. We have all heard the ego's voice as thought, injecting its negativity, fear, and drama into our lives. It perpetuates feelings of inadequacy and lack of self-worth. It overwhelms us with its constant judgment of self and others. It lacks truth and creates delusional dramas that trap us in the trance of forgetfulness that leads us to believe that we are separate from our True Divine identity. We get stuck in our head thinking obsessively about the past and the future and all the stories of life.

Our life becomes dominated by a set of false assumptions and stories that I call Soul Print Energy consciousness. All of what I am sharing with you has been taught to me by Jesus to help me understand the illusory and faulty thought system of the ego.

## INTUITION

The Soul Print Energy consciousness (SPEC) is also part of the ego illusion. This energy is all the negative faulty thoughts and beliefs about our self and others that has burdened mankind since the beginning of time. The ego is fed by and steeped in SPEC that is fraught with faulty beliefs such as, rejection, separation, abandonment, scarcity, darkness, and death etc. These are just energetic recycled stories and patterns of thinking and beliefs that lead us into an ingrained sense of victim consciousness and separation.

*The ego is a Divinely orchestrated faulty thought/belief system that is indispensible in setting the stage for this illusionary life experience. The ego voice is basically a hallucination. You can think of it as a thought system that is steeped in fear and lacking in Spiritual awareness. We hear this voice and its thoughts and mistakenly believe that it is our voice and truth.*

Although none of these aspects of the illusion are true, they are necessary in order to create the fabric of what we incorrectly think of as reality. We never really left our Divine Home. Somehow, we are participating in a dream life within the creative Consciousness that I call God. Pretty amazing, isn't it? It is like a 3D virtual energetic stage, a hologram, or a lucid dream if you will.

## REVIVING YOUR INTUITION

*We are Divine Consciousness
having a virtual human experience.*

Our Earth experience is a dream. It is God's stage of Creation on which the story of your life and the world is played out. God has created this energetic illusionary life with special care, just for you. It is God's theatre, and He has created every storyline. He gives a unique story and an awakening script to each of us.

As we get in touch with our intuition it paves the way back Home to our Creator's Love, healing, and Truth. Yet even as adults, many of us are stubborn and don't listen to our intuition. We may appear grown-up, more mature, but most of us have learned precious little about our Divine nature. As such, we have all experienced bouts of pain and trauma that ultimately stem from the belief that we are alone, separate from God.

The ego thought system steps in and takes control somewhere in childhood. Ego believes by imposing all its rules, prejudices, and judgments it is building a wall of safety and security around us. Unfortunately, snared within the ego's belief system we become gluttons for punishment and suffering when we incorporate all its faulty rules, stories, and judgments into our life.

Most of us are completely unaware that we are listening to a false sense of self, an unconscious and faulty belief system. If we accept the ego's false reality as truth it negates our wholeness, innocence, Divinity, eternal life, and protection.

This is all part of the human experience, living in a Spiritually unconscious trance of forgetfulness and not understanding the illusionary diverse details that accompany us through this incarnation journey.

This dream/illusion is complex and diverse. It includes our Divine Consciousness, unconsciousness, an inner child, the ego or shadow side, our will, the wounded parts of us, and SPEC. It is the sum of all these that, when blended, creates the illusion of a self and its perception of our human experience.

*The illusion is experienced in
our own mind/Consciousness...
we are Creation eternally creating dreams.*

This complex human experience is Divinely crafted and is Divine perfection even though it creates the illusion of fragmentation within our self and separation from God. The reawakening helps us remember that we are pure, innocent Spirit that can never really be hurt for we are One with God.

*God has no form. Yet, for this life
experience God has taken on all forms as
Conscious Creation...infinite imagination*

*and intelligence. There is Divine Consciousness in all things. Everything is God.*

We are pure Divine Consciousness experiencing its own creation of a self...like a character in a book or play. I know this can be enormously hard to conceptualize as we live each day tightly bound up in the illusion of our physical human existence. Over time, and with a dedicated Spiritual practice, openness, patience, persistence, and self-forgiveness, it all becomes easier to see and understand. We need self-forgiveness because we believe the illusion and judgments over Divine Truth, and this creates enormous amounts of suffering.

Forgiveness is a constant and indispensable part of our journey. It is the path to healing for yourself and for others. Truly, there is nothing really to forgive, but for this experience it is a great teacher of Grace, unconditional Love, and a necessary step in the expansion of our Consciousness.

Remember, our earthly experience is a dream. What I am describing to you is a myth of how the illusion works. This is the teaching given to me by Jesus as a way to try to understand our existence. It is a Divine mystery that we can never accurately describe or completely understand because we can never comprehend the expansiveness of God in this form. As we keep expanding in Consciousness, we receive updates to our Wisdom. Many times, they negate what we learned at an earlier stage of awakening. Divine Wisdom is revealed to us in stages because we cannot digest a more expansive Truth until we are ready to receive it.

What is it then that relentlessly drives us to keep seeking to understand how the mystery works? What irresistible force compels us to uncover the truth of our being? I believe it is the inextinguishable spark of Divine Spirit within. It is God calling us Home.

Led through life by the ego, we become experts in creating **adaptations, different versions of self** to cope with life. We split ourselves into so many parts that we keep getting further away from our True nature. Unknowingly, we rely on thinking errors and ineffective coping strategies to balance ourselves, but all they produce is a lack of internal self-awareness, feelings of self-rejection, self-abandonment, and a deeper feeling of separation from our Divine nature.

We concoct these adaptations because our thoughts and beliefs, along with societal and environmental influences are always forming, informing, or altering our perception of reality and who we are supposed to be.

All of this takes place because we believe we are separated from God. We are living and believing an illusion that is nothing more than a mirror of our Consciousness steeped in duality. A mirror of contrasting thoughts and beliefs. The result is that we essentially become a set of adaptations that create traits, coping mechanisms and behaviors that have nothing to do with the Truth of who we are.

These adaptations are premised on how we want or think family and society should see us rather than how God sees us. They are founded in experiences, faulty thinking, and beliefs that have been passed down through generations caught up in believing SPEC stories.

Yet, each of these adaptations is important throughout your journey. They help you become deeply entrenched in the illusion and become an integral part of the continuously unfolding story of you. No matter how your story plays out, what you do or don't do, does not change your Divine nature of innocence.

> *These adaptations also create the lack of intimacy that we experience in our relationships because we have not learned how to be intimate and honest with ourselves. We have no reference or understanding of our True nature as Love until that union is experienced with God.*

What I mean by intimacy with our Self is that we have not yet explored all the sum parts of our being, nor have we integrated them as part of our wholeness because we don't truly know who we are. It is also difficult to be honest with our self because we lack self-compassion, self-love, empathy, humor, and Divine Truth.

The illusion causes us to believe that we have been split into so many adaptations that we cannot find ourselves anymore. We are afraid to dig into the depths of who we really are because we have sorted all our traits, thoughts, experiences, and actions into good or bad. Most people feel unworthy and anticipate that they will not like what they find if they dig deep within.

For example, if you were brought up in a dysfunctional, negative environment, you might have developed strategies to avoid pain such as closing your heart, shutting down emotionally and physically, withholding love, being controlling, not committing to anyone, or trying to make others happy becoming a people pleaser. In a sense, you are filling the emptiness in your heart with numbness, so you do not have to feel, but your feelings are extremely important.

You might believe those strategies work, but they don't. All they do is create more separation from others and from your Self. You gain little and lose out on so much. All this pain and loss comes from not remembering your Divine nature, forgetting that you have an infinite amount of Love within you and that you are always Divinely perfect and protected.

We have many role models that teach us ineffective strategies for getting through life. They come from family and friends who have been laboring under the same faulty SPEC beliefs. The problem is that we are not learning any Truth from within. We are steeped in faulty beliefs and are constantly ***searching outside our self for the wisdom to understand our experience of life rather then searching within.***

We are creatures of habits and patterns, and our trance mind is like a tape recorder that keeps replaying the same thoughts, feelings, and behaviors in response to any and every scenario we encounter in life.

The faulty beliefs and experiences are engrained in our memory. Our patterned responses begin to form our expectations of what life will bring us. We then fall into a cycle of repeatedly manifesting those negative expectations, endlessly calling-in more and more of the same energetic patterns, hence the rerun of suffering situations and experiences. Yet, although it is painful there is a purpose to all of this. It is to heal and awaken.

We speak terrible things over our selves. We tell ourselves that we are ill or going to catch something. We tell ourselves that we don't have enough, that we are unworthy, that we can't do this or that, that life sucks, we're getting older and that nothing ever goes our way. No wonder we don't want to stay present when we are unwittingly creating a life that **FEELS** terribly painful always reaching for doom!

I can go on and on about how we speak negativity rather than well-being, love, happiness, and abundance into our lives. We become the creator of what we experience, the good, the bad, and the ugly. This is all the result of our believing the stories and illusions of the SPEC. Our perceptions and beliefs keep creating more external experiences and continues the story.

We keep replaying and reliving the same patterns of external experiences that are the product of all the faulty thoughts, feelings, and beliefs that we've been accumulating since our earliest childhood. It's the same kind of thing that results from traumatic experiences. In a sense, we all have Post Traumatic Stress Disorder, but most of us are simply unaware of it. We keep re-traumatizing ourselves.

These repetitive patterns are an energetic illusion; like a memory that keeps playing over and over again in ever changing situations and circumstances as you grow and mature. They are patterns that keep appearing throughout the course of your life because they need to be healed, processed, and released.

You need to stop believing and buying into your stories of victimization. That means your perceptions of your experiences need to change. As you gradually learn how to stop *reacting* to these patterns their power will diminish.

You will have experiences within the normal course of your day that trigger you to re-experience the same internal thoughts and feelings that then generate the same external responses that you've been learning and employing ever since early childhood.

Various people, relationships, situations, circumstances, and experiences generally trigger these patterns and responses. They produce the same kinds of feelings and emotions just as they did when you were a child.

Let's discuss perception and story creation on a deeper level. All creations start with a 'thought.' Whether it is faulty or not is not the issue because the sequence of your automatic chain reaction to a thought is the same. Intertwined with each thought is a perception about it. These perceptions can be positive, negative, good, or bad. They may be triggered by something you have experienced in the external world or simply by a random thought that you have. This perception starts a myriad of additional thoughts. You begin to build a story around the original thought that typically creates some kind of drama.

Next comes a feeling from the very story you just created. From those feelings comes a reaction or response that often leads you to believe that you are suffering in some way. You don't even realize that you are creating your own suffering. It is all happening in your mind. Nothing is happening outside of you.

*Thought's cause >Perception's cause > Feeling's cause >Reactions*

Your perceptions are coming from your old programming, beliefs, and experiences. They shape the very story you are swept up in and believe to be true. Most of the time that story is not true. This thought process is happening all day long triggered by your own thoughts, ego thoughts, what you see, hear or experience. The constant bombardment and clutter of false stories is what keeps you anchored in faulty beliefs about yourself. These, in turn, exacerbate feelings of victim consciousness and unworthiness. With all of this nonsense going on in your head there is no room for you to see the Love and Light that you truly are.

*You are only reacting to your own creative stories and none of them are founded in reality, yet they are creating your life experience.*

Therefore, it is so important not to attach to faulty thoughts or speak negativity over yourself or others because it shapes your external reality. At the same time there are thoughts coming from God, your Intuition, that are creating your day for you, steering you towards how your day is to be played out. You believe them to be your own thoughts. God's thoughts are always trying to create joy in you. It is up to you to receive those thoughts and attach to them. Your reaction to what you think you are experiencing is the only true power you have. You choose how to perceive each moment.

When I can catch an ego thought happening in my mind, I try to head it off right away. I remind myself that it is not a true thought and to let it go as if it were just 'spam.' Delete. I do not go further into perception. This stops the chain reaction. The ability to do this takes great practice, patience and presence in discerning which thoughts are real and those that are not.

Although I have become greatly attuned to the thoughts in my mind it does not mean that I never fall prey to an ego thought and start creating a story. At times I feel like I am under siege from the story in my mind and truly I am only stuck in a delusional story. I am happy to say that I catch myself much quicker than I ever had in the past.

I have been keenly aware of the themes of ego thought in my mind. The themes are abandonment, rejection, attack, fear of illness or medical conditions, getting physically hurt, getting scammed, betrayal, not good enough, someone is taking advantage of me, people will get mad at me, being hypocritical about myself, scarcity, fear of missing out, I don't count or matter, I can't make anyone happy, etc. For the most part our stories are filled with suffering or visions of grandeur. Sounds like Bipolar Disorder, doesn't it? It's not; it is all caused by listening to ego thoughts.

One of the major themes of my story is betrayal by family. What I have come to realize is that I assigned guilt to my family for hurting me. Since I awakened, I have been working on forgiving others and myself. I try to see each person as innocent, that they are just playing a role in my story for healing and awakening purposes. I realize that I am just projecting my own guilt and judgment onto them. I forgot my own innocence, my Divine nature and became a judge. The Truth is that everything we see is Consciousness in creative form.

I thought I had overcome judgement of my family; however, the ego is tricky and hides the fact that there is still more forgiveness to be had. The ego lives in denial. It wants to hold onto the belief that it is always right. It does not want to face the truth; it only wants to condemn others which is the same thing as condemning you. It is an ongoing process to detach from old stories, beliefs, and behaviors.

You think your heart is wide open, but it is not. You need to take one day at a time, healing as you are ready, deeper and deeper, each step letting go of what no longer serves you. The goal is to detach from ego thoughts that are deeply rooted in your belief system.

All these themes arise from SPEC. We all share similar themes we just experience them at different intensities based on our storyline. Belief in these faulty thoughts challenges us to create coping skills and defense mechanisms which in turn create adaptations to our character or persona. Most of these skills and mechanisms are not healthy or positive, they are counterproductive. This is all done to hide shame and guilt. They are the outcome of believing faulty thoughts. This is how we all constructed a false sense of self.

For example: obsessive compulsive disorder is experienced at different degrees based on each individual. It is a coping skill individually created to ward off fearful thoughts. The thinking behind the coping skill is 'if I do 'something' it will counteract or ward off the fearful thought I just had, so it doesn't come true. The 'something' is typically a repetitive behavior or thought. You are not even aware that you have constructed such a coping mechanism; it just happens. Then it becomes a habit like an addiction. This had been one of my coping skills.

I can tell by the way I am feeling that I am stuck in a delusion from SPEC and ask God to help me unwind or let go of what I created. I ask to be centered back in Truth, Love & Peace. It always works. I receive an immediate shift in perception that is conceived in the highest Light. We are so intimately Loved and guided, and you experience it when you ask for help from within.

From the time of our birth, we are intently tuned-in to our internal world of needs…the need for Love, warmth, food, comfort, safety, etc. We are also intimately connected to our Divinity; we remember who we truly are. Babies are pure joy. But as babies and young children we can't satisfy these needs by ourselves. We quickly learn how to gain attention to get those needs met by others. As we grow older these strategies become ingrained in us, they become automatic, and we gradually become less in-tuned to our Divine Self.

In our quest to have our needs met externally we can detach from our intuition and Knowingness. Self-rejection and self-abandonment can easily take hold as early as childhood or as a teenager. Challenges arise as we respond to life based on societal expectations and the dictates of others.

A pattern of disregard for our self may also develop because of witnessing how others failed to properly take care of themselves. Maybe our parents took care of us well enough, but never took care of their own emotional, Spiritual or physical well-being. How many of us witnessed our parents worrying incessantly because they never learned to rely on our Creator to lead them? Unfortunately, they were stuck in the trance too.

Regardless of the underlying causes, the result is that we become detached from our Knowingness. Our intuition and internal Wisdom no longer carry the same weight and we do not know how to care for ourselves emotionally with compassionate self-love. We forgot the Divine Loving nature and pure goodness that we are.

All children need love and attention. Maybe you had parents that were so stressed and overwhelmed by their own issues that they did not know how to give you the love and attention you needed. If you did not receive the love and attention you needed, it may be that you began to feel that you were unworthy and not entitled to receive it. When this occurs children generally respond in one of the following ways. They may become overly needy, avoidant or they may develop behavior problems.

Perhaps you had 'helicopter parents' who took care of everything for you and never taught you how to care or make decisions for your self. This kind of experience in childhood can lead to self- rejecting behavior from a lack of self-confidence or learned helplessness.

For example, when you get hurt physically or emotionally do you tell yourself it is nothing? Do you push through the pain rather than stopping to acknowledge it and take care of yourself or change what you're doing?

Many of us were not taught how to self-soothe, and therefore we look to others or things to do it for us. That's how addictive behaviors arise. We don't believe that we can take good care of ourselves emotionally, physically or Spiritually. When you learn how to reconnect with your intuition, to God, all the lack you feel within yourself is repaired and transformed. You have great healing qualities. God teaches you how to self-soothe and how to unconditionally Love yourself with such compassion and grace, it brings you to tears of joy.

We diminish our Knowingness whenever we allow our ego and others to make decisions for us. The ego never makes decisions based on what is best for us Spiritually.

It makes a priority of our external, temporal needs rather than our internal, Spiritual ones.

The ego is focused on performance, appearances, validation, getting love, things, having everything under control and being safe. It couldn't care less about our Spiritual needs or our connection to God because the ego doesn't believe in a Creator that provides Love, protection, and all the other things that we feel are missing in our life. However, there appears to be a Spiritual side to the ego that you become aware of during the awakening process. It thinks the work its doing is what is transforming you rather then God itself. It uses the Divine Knowledge to bolster itself in the eyes of others. The ego can be very tricky at times.

The ego only believes in itself. It is laser-focused on appearances and societal expectations because it believes that theses are the things that will keep us safe and make us happy. The ego takes full credit as long as our life appears to be successful. When we encounter challenges in our life the ego immediately abdicates any sense of responsibility and readily blames everyone and everything other than itself for our difficulties.

But the opposite is true, we are responsible for everything we think, feel, do, or say. We are responsible for the life that we create and how we perceive and live it. We all have this power. The real power is in perceiving everything through the lens of Divine Truth.

We experience externally what we think, believe, and say to our selves, therefore it is critical to perceive, believe and speak only Divine Truth from our awakened Self. This Self recognizes its innocence and understands that our Being is always guided and moved by God. Therefore, we should never judge ourselves; God is always in control... and this includes our transformation as well.

*The Earth stage is a mirror reflection of the level of our Consciousness. We create a belief in separation because we perceive life through an illusion of duality (Heaven & Earth). Our mind then perceives through a lens of doubt and conflict. We see the world and ourselves in terms of good, bad, or neutral. Truthfully, there is no separation or conflict. There is only One Divine reality; it is Love.*

All these complex adaptations and fears lead us to believe that we are not a whole integrated being. Through the process of awakening, we come to believe that we must integrate our body, mind, and Soul. Yet, as our Consciousness expands, we realize that we are already wholly integrated as the essence of God. The good news is that we are whole right at this very moment and will be so throughout eternity. All it takes is **believing** Divine Truth over everything else.

## INTUITION

*We can only gain this intimate relationship with our Self by having an intimate relationship with God. He teaches us how to Love every part of our Self and what our True nature is.*

Intuitive skills do not vary from person to person; we are all the same Consciousness. We all must develop our Spiritual muscles and skills, and that takes time. It is critical to remember that we are not cultivating these skills alone…God is always helping us ascend by expanding our Consciousness. In fact, He is doing all the work, we just need to be in receiving mode and accept that transformation happens within a Divine timeline.

You are still One with God, asleep or awake; that never changes. This dream is just an 'Earth story.' You are now starting to understand why you drifted into forgetfulness. No worries, God will wake you up at your special time, but you can get a jump on your awakening if you start seeking and questioning your existence from within.

In the meantime, I want you to understand that everything that has happened in your life is perfect and in Divine order. There is absolutely nothing wrong with you or what you have experienced, created, or done. You are always Perfection in motion.

*You have done absolutely nothing wrong.
You are perfect right where you are
in every moment.*

"*You did not create this illusion, Debbie, it was created for you. This is the role you have been casted for. There needs to be drama and everything else to make the movie real and interesting. God is the creator of everything, you, and all parts of the illusion. However, God's Love is the only thing that exists.*"
- *Jesus* -

Journal Entry
Easter Sunday 4/5/2015
With Jesus and my Inner Child

**My Inner Child talking to me:** I love you. You are a child of God. You are precious, Divine, and worthy. It is God's Joy to see you happy and in love with your life. But what is life? Most of us do not know what that is. It is all the love in your heart that gets scattered and given away or locked away so no one, not even you, can feel it. We were made to feel that Love and share it with others. We forget that is why God created us. Very simply, it's just Love…yet it can be one of the hardest things to accomplish. Some hearts are fresh and have not been tainted, therefore, those people can feel and give to others, but most have stopped this flow of loving energy even to themselves.

We want to help people fall in love with themselves, with God and others. To do this we must learn how to evolve our heart, into our highest. We do this by helping others and helping ourselves. We must see through the illusions of life that Love is the ultimate answer to everything. We must rescue our heart in order to move forward. God rescues our hearts, but only if we allow Him. He calls on us daily to see and hear. We have learned not to listen or see all the miracles He has created around us.

We are asleep and unconscious. We wake up and get a glimmer of the Truth, then we go back to sleep all the while yearning for the Love and happiness that is right in our very being. It is amazing and it is sad. We resist help. We stop the flow. The energy is always there within. We feel helpless, as if we were blind. It is so powerful and moving to watch.

**Me:** Why do we do this?

**My Inner Child:** We do it because we feel grief and loss from the illusion of being separated from God's Love. But the Truth is that we are never separated from God. We never were and never will be. We feel those things for no true reason. We are children looking to everyone and everything else to fill us with Love. We forget who we are, where we came from, and focus on things that don't matter and cannot take the pain and fear away, yet we continue to do it. It is a blessing and a misery.

Being in denial, an illusion can help us feel that we are not in pain, but it is untrue. Ultimately, it brings more misery to our hearts…the loneliness of not knowing God's Love. God gave us our will and that will is exceedingly strong. It is so strong that it keeps us locked in these trances. Our trance can only be unlocked through God's Love, yet we keep escaping back to old ways and old habits that do not work for us, Debbie. It is imperfection at its finest. This is what being human is about. We are lost in a world out of touch with why we are here.

**Me:** What can we do?

**My Inner Child:** We can let go and let God take over. It sounds easy but it isn't. All the neediness of life keeps dragging us down…wanting things, thinking they will make us happy. True happiness comes from within. Even if we have all our desires met, what good is it if we do not feel happy? We are clear about what does not make us happy, yet we continue to do things that continue this pain. Humans are amazing creatures of habit.

**Me:** Jesus, what is it that we are writing? What is my Inner Child trying to tell me?

**Jesus:** It is a Soul Print.

**Me:** What is that?

**Jesus:** It is the energetic story that our Souls carry around that contains the misbeliefs about ourselves, what humans call Karma …we need to change and overcome these misbeliefs.

**Me:** Where did this Soul Print come from?

**Jesus:** It's inherited energy. Thoughts, beliefs, and experiences that have been passed down to us through generations of suffering and strong wills. When God gave us free will it was to be used for good and love. Unfortunately, our Soul Print suffering has caused the will to be used in unimaginably destructive ways.

**Me:** God must have known this.

**Jesus:** Yes, but He has given everyone a Loving heart and knows that if the heart is followed it will prevail.

**Me:** Today I heard the story of Cain and Able. Why was Cain suffering and why did he want to kill Able? Where did the suffering come from?

**Jesus:** He was filled with resentment when he believed God rejected his sacrifice. He did not understand God in his heart because his ego and will were in control. The sacrificing of the lamb is just a metaphor for allowing yourself to show up vulnerable, to surrender and align with the Love of God's goodness, through trust and faith, just as I have done. *There is no sacrifice for God's Love or goodness, Debbie, it is just given. One needs to just be open to it, allow it, and receive it.*

**Me:** So, this has been an affliction since the beginning of man? Cain must have felt awfully rejected, jealous and angry and felt entitled to blame Abel for it. There are so many lessons in this one story of suffering. I actually see all of the patterns of Soul Print energy in this one story.

**Jesus:** Yes, there has been so much suffering in this world since the beginning of time. Fear, darkness, separation, lack of safety, they all were and still are problems. These misperceptions have been with man since the beginning. They are like a fierce energy living inside of him.

**Me:** This story you are telling me, is it just for me or for others?

**Jesus:** It is how I want you to understand our world. You will need this to understand people better. Most people act out of fear, just like you, but it does not have to affect you if you understand it has nothing to do with you. If you understand this, it will positively affect the way you see yourself and others. It needs to change. Your heart needs to absorb this knowledge so you can grow more.

**Me:** I understand. We are all fearful of many things, some more than others, but we all experience fear. I am not to judge it.

**Jesus:** Yes, not to judge it within yourself or when you see it in others.

**Me:** So, when I am confused and don't understand how I am feeling or what to do, is it okay?

**Jesus:** Yes, it is okay and there's nothing wrong with it. That is why you come to God to help you with your pain and confusion and to help you with the answers. No one else can do this for you. This is why you bring us to your client therapy sessions. You are there to comfort them and to reflect what they are feeling is okay. ***God will heal them if they allow it. You cannot heal them.*** If this is not the time for their healing, then you just provide comfort.

**Me:** What else is there for me to know, to focus on? What will make me happy? What fills my Soul with passion?

**Jesus:** Good question. Singing, dancing, telling stories, having fun, loving others, being in or near the water, art, travel, and new experiences. You like movement and you are stuck in keeping still.

**Me:** How do I mix my Soul's purpose of being loving and a comfort to others with my Soul's passion?

**Jesus:** Try dancing in synchronicity to the story of God's Love so that you can feel the love and passion through movement. Let yourself be swept away by the grace and movement and the feelings of Love that fulfill your Soul. It is beautiful.

**Me:** How do I learn this story or dance?

# INTUITION

**Jesus:** You already know the story and you feel it in every part of you, but you stop yourself, you don't let go, you are reserved and fearful of judgment. When you let go it will come.

**Me:** How do I let go?

**Jesus:** Practice, go in your room, close the door, put music on and dance.

**Me:** Is there a teacher or someone to help me let go with my body, mind & Spirit?

**Jesus:** It is already happening through massage.

**Me:** What kind of music?

**Jesus:** You will Know it when you hear it.

Jesus showed me visually during meditation what kind of dancing he was talking about. I would describe this as a free-form type of dance. Very slow dance movements to relaxing music. It is wonderful and I love it, yet my ego and will are always challenging me, trying to distract me from doing it.

Just an aside, my inner child shares with me delightful children's stories about God. Someday they will be published so I can share them with you.

---

Journal Entry 1/12/17
Meditation with John the Baptist

---

**John:** Your meditation and journal time is sacred and Holy, Debbie. It is the way you worship the Love and Light. It nourishes you. It is a time to learn and integrate. There is nothing more loving you can do for yourself than to give yourself this time. It expands you and connects you with the Love and life force that flows within you and everything else. It is a time for purification and centering. See it as worship, the same way others would go to a church or temple to hear the word of God, although that word flows through you.

God's word is full of Divine Knowledge, Light, guidance and Love for your specific journey. It keeps pulling you in to remember who you truly are. Daily practice is essential. Within you is the Holy temple that is filled with Love, the Spiritual energy of the Universe wanting to guide you. Your meditation time is a daily reassurance that lets you know that you are on the right path. The Love and growth bring you one step closer to experiencing your wholeness. There is no replacement for your daily meditation. This is your sanctuary. It is a space of Divine Love.

We are writing this to let others know that they need to do the same. Daily meditation provides important internal guidance. It helps us let go of the habit of looking outside of our self for guidance. No one else knows your curriculum or itinerary for your Spiritual journey but you and your Spiritual guides. Others can give you pieces of the puzzle but not the itinerary or curriculum. They are not a substitute for experiencing the Oneness of Love within.

**Me:** Can I ask what my itinerary is? (I feel my ego creeping in with fear. I breathe and release it).

**John:** Good, that was perfect in diminishing your fear. Yes, first off, your itinerary is to be happy and enjoy your life. Second, you were given several gifts and talents that need to be allowed to develop and be polished. Your message from us is very important and needs to be carried out, such as your books, your posts and public speaking. This will get easier in time; you will continue growing and so will your message. You have been chosen to bring a beautiful message of hope and Love. We need to keep working with you to refine it and to also help you integrate it so that you are feeling all the Love, support, and peace that you can. It is a mighty message to deliver, and we chose you because you can do it like no one else can. You have immense strength, focus and passion to help others awaken. You are such a blessing, Debbie, and you need to see it.

**Me:** You are so loving, John. Thank you.

**John:** I know you are tired, and this is not sinking in yet, but it will. You already are creating beautiful things and there is much more to come.

**Me:** Is there anything else about my itinerary?

**John:** You will continue to unfold with more grace. You will get to do amazing things that you have been hoping for. Be gentle with yourself, you are a beautiful being.

INTUITION

Journal Entry 8/25/18
With God

**Me:** I don't want to be stubborn anymore, God.

**God:** You are not stubborn, Debbie, you are beautiful. The stubbornness is the ego in protection mode. We do not want to demonize the ego. You have felt conflict lately with others who believe the ego is negative. You have been trying to not view the ego as bad, understanding that it serves many purposes including giving momentum and movement to all your creations. It is I, God, who created the ego and the illusion for you to have a fun experience. You need to remember, Debbie, that the ego is part of the illusion of life. It is not real; it is a faulty thought system. It is just a part of your illusionary experience and although you are purely Divine, you need to integrate this understanding of ego into your human experience.

**Me:** Some people still look at the ego as something terrible, like I used to.

**God:** I don't want you to align with the thought that the ego is terrible. That belief is not helpful. Do you remember when you saw your eighteen- and twenty-year-old self as the ego and wanted to metaphorically kill those parts of you?

**Me:** Yes, I remember that God. It was awful. It was when I was working on healing those parts of me. I had so much self-hatred.

**God:** There is no part of you or anything within the illusion that is "bad." Things are just judged or perceived as bad. These are misperceptions. As your highest form you judge nothing as "bad." Do you understand, Debbie?

**Me:** Yes, I do. Can the ego go higher, God? Jesus told me that the ego couldn't communicate with the Higher Self.

**God:** The ego does not go higher. It is you that has mastered staying more present and have become a witness to your internal world without judging the ego. It is true, Debbie, the ego cannot communicate with Higher Consciousness, it is not real. It is YOU that must start appreciating the role that ego energy plays, therefore, there will be no more conflict with it.

## INTUITION

*You are still getting upset because you drift off into unconsciousness and continue to judge yourself for it. You then become frustrated with yourself and the ego. It then becomes an illusionary battle within because you feel that you need to 'win.' It is not necessary to be frustrated just keep shifting yourself back to Me.*

The ego is part of a growth process, an expansion in your Consciousness. Accept and embrace the ego as you call it an 'illusionary energetic travel partner', as a helper of understanding contrast. *It is not in opposition to you. You do not have to overcome it or beat it. All you must do is be aware of those thoughts and not believe them.* You stay in a higher vibration by not judging yourself, the ego or getting frustrated with it. It is only helping you grow in mastering yourself energetically, consciously. The lesson at hand is learning to love all parts of you, this incarnation, and seeing this magical life experience as fun.

*Your Spiritual journey is a life of Spiritual Self-discovery planned by you and God together as One. You are playing a 'character role' and self-discovery helps you learn what is behind the character.*
-Jesus-

## Divine Revelation
## A message from God

Divine revelation is an awareness of Divine Wisdom. It is Divine Truth that makes its way into your Consciousness. It is I, God, revealing Myself to you.

I am speaking to you all the time. Some will hear Wisdom from within and others will simply feel and Know it. It is a holy moment when Divine revelation takes over all other perspectives…when the veil of your unconsciousness is lifted, and you see things through Divine eyes. You are given an awareness or Knowingness that you have not had before, a deeper level of perception, or a more expansive view of a Divine Truth of which you had but little understanding.

I am helping you understand your journey each step of the way. At precise moments I help you have more clarity about yourself, others, the Divine mystery that is your life and its inseparable connection with Me. Your life is a journey of co-creation with Me. It is a journey of understanding your experiences on a Spiritual level, a level that can be difficult to attain if you stay bound by the limitations of your physical senses and subdued by the domination of your ego.

My revelation will come to you gradually, quietly, as you spend more time with Me, close to Me, conversing with Me, experiencing Me, and understanding the Oneness of

## INTUITION

all Creation. It may come to you through the whispered words that you hear when you are attentive to the rhythms of Nature, through a person, a friend, or a life situation, anything that gives birth to a heightened internal awareness that allows Me to shift you to a higher perspective.

I am always guiding you whether you hear Me or are simply aware of My presence. Many call this sense of awareness, intuition. Intuition is a connection with Divine Wisdom in which you are prompted to know something or to take action. Intuition comes from our universal connectedness, our Oneness.

Everyone has intuitive abilities, but many do not recognize that when intuition brings Divine revelation, a higher understanding, the source of that deep intuitive feeling or Knowingness is Me. Tied to their earthly senses, their powers of thought, analysis and their ego, they believe they figured something out on their own or that the lesson learned was simply the end product of a series of life experiences. But this isn't true.

You are not living this life separate and alone. You can never be separated from Me for we are taking this journey together as One. Over time you will understand more. Divine revelation will never cease to be given to you for it is your task to awaken to the Truth of who you are, One with Me, Divine Love remembering itself.

## Chapter Four

THE NATURAL STATE OF BEING IS LOVE

*Self-love is a process that requires the integration of Knowing who you truly are.*

In the last chapter we saw how very easy it is for us to shift from intuition to ego, from Consciousness to unconsciousness as we Spiritually mature.

The drift to unconsciousness occurs all too easily. This is what I call being in the trance. You need to develop a practice, a willingness to stay ever present. Yet, as you drift away from Consciousness you are always receiving a gentle nudge from God to help you refocus back to present time. I have always asked for help from God to stay present, this springs from my willingness to participate in a co-creation. Whether you acknowledge God's gentle prompting is up to you. There may be times when you simply choose to remain unconsciousness and that's okay.

# INTUITION

*When we are present, we are open to God's Grace that helps us to shift our perception of what we think, believe, see, or experience. In fact, this whole life's journey is learning how to perceive through a Divine lens rather than the ego's thought system.*

*It is so comforting to know that God is always leading you Home to reawaken you to the One Conscious mind that you share with Him.*

*The waffling back and forth between Consciousness and unconsciousness is normal and part of the awakening process. As our Consciousness expands, we become more adept at staying present and in loving control (Divinely perceiving) of the many aspects of our human experience.*

Until we master the art of staying present, the ego voice dominates us through its constant focus on thoughts of fear, lack and past experiences. Our intuition guides us through Love, abundance and Wisdom steeped in Divine Truth. These are two distinctly different thoughts to follow.

Both options are always available, and it is always our choice of which voice we listen to. Understand that the ego thought system is filled with contrast and conflict.

## THE NATURAL STATE OF BEING IS LOVE

Divine Wisdom, your intuition, is a higher awareness that helps you navigate the illusion from a higher, expanded perception. When we are listening to our intuition, we will always make the decisions and choices that are best for us even if we don't understand the outcome of the choice at times. Sometimes those outcomes don't always turn out as we expected. We don't always know what's in our Divine best interest.

*I am free...free to choose how to perceive and experience this life anyway I want.*
*Let it be in joy!*

We make choices all day long. Unfortunately, most of our choices are made at the direction of the ego. Ego gains control early on in our lives when SPEC and family and societal programing appears to sever our connection with our Divinity, our True identity. The illusory trance basically buries our Truth under the influence of the daily drama generated by ego. As we master the art of staying present, we recognize that ego will often try to disguise itself as the voice of our intuition. Its deception can be subtle or abrupt.

Even so, within the illusion all is accounted for and in Divine Order. *God has given each of us an Earth story. From that we build an image of who we are and what our life is about.* We each have been given the same ego and SPEC and those energies play out brilliantly, yet relentlessly, as they intermingle and create your personal storyline.

God is always in complete control, because we are never separated from His Consciousness and His goodness. We may think and feel that we are on our own, but we are never separated from God regardless of our storyline or experiences. There is no right or wrong. There is no good or bad. It is our choice whether to awaken in this lifetime or not. However, if you want a more joyful and happy life it is time to awaken.

Think of your present self as though you were standing in some middle space between Consciousness and ego. The trance that dominates us makes us feel that there is a gap, a separation, a duality between that which is Divine and all things of this Earth. That feeling or belief is just an illusion.

The trance is an energetic pull like gravity that keeps drawing you into unconsciousness. Therefore, you have difficulty staying present. This illusionary gap is where the ego and SPEC play out their roles. Ego wants to keep you ensnared in the trance with all its faulty beliefs and keeps you mired in forgetfulness.

The trance and its *delusions* are all that the ego knows. Awakening shatters your illusionary trance and teaches you to remember and *believe* who you truly are, pure God-Consciousness and nothing else. There is no gap, no

## THE NATURAL STATE OF BEING IS LOVE

separation. You are the mind of God, Divine Consciousness, creating and experiencing infinite Creation.

Nonetheless, you do need some anchoring into the illusion. You can't just sit in a corner waiting for enlightenment and not experience your life. There is a role for you to play in this world that is very important and created just for you. You have specific lessons to learn, and you have a destiny to fulfill; it is your Divine appointment.

We can think of our self as Spirit (Consciousness) dreaming that we are human. As part of that dream our Spirit purposefully forgets that it is creatively dreaming, and the ego and SPEC take over as we enter the trance.

*The trance keeps us stuck in our head constantly thinking, planning, projecting and fearing.*

It is all too easy for us to remain stuck in our head to block out all of the distractions, interactions and pain of life. Before we know it, we become addicted to staying in the trance and we find ourselves spending more time in this space rather than being in the present.

The trance is a comfortable familiar place where we do not have to face being present and deal with what is bothering us. It keeps us out of Conscious reality and allows all the faulty programming, thinking, difficult past experiences and beliefs to come alive and beat us down. This is where all the delusional trauma/drama, blame and victim stories are created and acted out. We are creating from a lower level or vibration of Consciousness.

Awakening creates motivation to do the work of staying present and searching within to find our way back Home. Now it is time for us to take loving compassionate control of all the diversity within by mastering our internal world guided by Divine Truth. Through this Earth experience, we will always have the ego thought system to deal with, but the ego will be much less powerful as we gradually stop choosing to listen or believe it. Understand that the ego thoughts are intended to help us break patterns of faulty beliefs.

When we understand this, we come into alignment with our True identity. We do this by staying present as much as possible, ***believing*** our Divine Truth, owning who we are and not what the ego tells us.

Through meditation you can reconnect and refocus your attention on your intuition. You ask from your open heart to have God reveal Himself to you. Eventually you understand that you are always in complete alignment with God, you have just been listening to and perceiving life through the ego thought system rather than Divine Perfection. You have never left Home although you think you have...***you are simply believing that you are a distinct, independent self, living a human life.***

## THE NATURAL STATE OF BEING IS LOVE

You can return Home to God any moment of the day to learn more Truth about the illusion and yourself. You will have your own Truth with God since your journey is individual to you. However, your natural state of being is Love and Joy for that is God's state of being and this is the only Truth that eventually everyone comes to understand. You no longer have to believe ego thoughts. God replaces them with Divine Truth. He is always correcting your thought process; it is the voice of Divine reason.

Believing God's Truth is a process. Even as you expand in your awakened Consciousness you will find that believing ego thoughts is easier than believing the Truth that comes from God. You have been listening to lies and have been deceived by ego for a very long time, but the shift in beliefs will eventually come and when it does the peace that engulfs you within is pure bliss.

God's Will is for you to be happy and joyful. You achieve this by having an intimate relationship with Him and learning and believing your True nature. God is always in control of you since you are One. When you finally believe you are One and the same you no longer have internal arguments as if there were two or more of you.

This recognition of course takes time. Your awakening is a work in progress that continues to deepen throughout your life. As your Consciousness keeps expanding you come to understand that there really is no battle within or without; it is all simply part of the illusion that is inextricably embedded within your Consciousness.

One of the most intriguing parts of the illusion is the myth that we exist in a world governed by time and space. There is no such thing as time or space. All of our lives, past, present and future, are being played out at once.

> *There is only one point of existence and that is eternity. Eternity is always NOW.*
> *-Jesus-*

We are baby, toddler, child, teen-ager, young adult, and older adult, born and deceased all at once. All these stages of Consciousness, programing and experience are active in the energetic illusion, and they are constantly merging and converging within us as we evolve, to help us heal and awaken.

We all have unhealed wounded parts of ourselves, very often from our childhood, that have been surreptitiously controlling us through faulty beliefs and actions. This is why our old wounds are triggered so easily. It is why we keep revisiting the same patterns and problems repeatedly through scenarios/situations that the SPEC brings us. Our lives are filled with energetic memories, thinking and behavioral patterns that need to be healed and perceived differently.

## THE NATURAL STATE OF BEING IS LOVE

Only God can manage all this diversity with Love and compassion. He teaches us to become the Divinely matured parent filled with unconditional Love for our entire illusionary complex Self.

*The healing process begins when we start to examine, process, and correct our faulty thinking, beliefs, and misperceptions about our experiences and who we are. When we stop believing the lies the healing is completed. In fact, all we ever needed to be truly healed is to overcome the belief that we are separate from God.*

Can you see how this SPEC-driven life experience not only causes you to forget your nature, but destroys any understanding of who you are and how much you are loved? This is what disconnects you from loving your Self. Enormous damage is done to your self-esteem when you don't remember your Oneness or that Love and Joy are your essence.

You must recognize your True worth and learn how to *fall in love* with yourself again. This cannot occur unless you allow God to build an intimate relationship with you founded in trust and unconditional Love. God teaches you Love because that is all that He is which means that is all that you are. Love is always extending itself.

## INTUITION

Our essence remains unhurt and unblemished because it is God Consciousness and is always safe at Home. It never forgets this, even during the trance of our virtual experience through life as a human. The awakening allows us to become Divinely conscious again. Now we can start living from Truth rather than victim stories.

We get so excited when we feel the first soft kiss of Divine awakening even though the trance keeps pulling us back into forgetfulness. *It is like having a moment of clarity in the midst of a Spiritual amnesia.* The awakening is completely new to us, but within our Higher Consciousness we have always known our True nature. It knows us intimately, completely, because we are One and the same, inseparable, indivisible, pure Divine Love.

Imagine! We believe we are completely cut off from this pure Love and inner Wisdom only getting glimpses of it now and then until we awaken to realize *we are One with God*. Fascinating, isn't it? Realizing we are One with God is the initial revelation but moving from realization to true acceptance of our Oneness with God is another gradual process that we must work our way through.

There is nothing else but God Consciousness. The energetic illusion of our body, ego, trance, SPEC, and life was created for us to have fun on the virtual stage of our earthly experience. The beautiful Love of God is waiting to help us reconnect, remember, and embrace our Divinity. We forgot we have a direct connection to God

## THE NATURAL STATE OF BEING IS LOVE

who is always ready and willing to respond. We just need to ask and then **take the time to listen.**

*When we live under the influence of the ego's illusion of control, we are blinded and appear to be cut off from our Divine reality.*

We're unable to hear God's voice, because we have accepted the illusion of separation and the belief that we are in control of our destiny. Neither is true. It is important to understand that God is good and only wants the best for us and has everything, including the details of our lives, in Divine order and control.

We are Divine Consciousness having a virtual dream. That dream is the story of our life here on Earth written by you and God. But it is nothing more than a dream, nothing more than an illusion that feels completely real. Wrapped in the illusion we falsely believe we are experiencing a physical existence. Even though we are only experiencing an illusion it all seems so real that it creates an urgency to keep doing and controlling rather than allowing our dream life to unfold in accordance with God's plan.

*What's even more fascinating is that you are the Creator because there is only One Consciousness. You created your dream and forgot. Finding God is finding your True Self.*

# INTUITION

*You are the Creator and its creation.*

When we are awakened and guided by God/intuition we can then be prompted to the next steps of our lives without fear, anxiety, and urgency, knowing our life is unfolding in God's hands. We are witnessing our life as though we were experiencing a lucid dream. When we are Divinely awakened, we become aware that our experience of this Earthly existence is nothing more than a dream.

Part of our Earth story is that we reincarnate. As such, we believe that our life is a rerun playing repeatedly throughout eternity, each life involving different stories, different settings, different physical bodies, etc. We keep getting multiple chances to awaken and perceive life differently, which can lead us into breaking faulty belief patterns and return Home to a more expansive level of Consciousness.

When you awaken you suddenly realize that you are an actor following the script of your own creation. Whether you are awake or not you still view the same script. The difference is that as you begin to awaken you can perceive life and yourself differently. This gradually shifts your storyline from being immersed in an illusion of victim consciousness to a much more peaceful and enjoyable life as you live in Oneness with God.

## THE NATURAL STATE OF BEING IS LOVE

Just think, we all have God's intuitive power and Wisdom within us to make excellent choices and to create and do what is best for us. Unfortunately, we don't always remember that we have this creative power and don't know how to access it or trust it.

To access and activate that power we must awaken and start the process of learning how to focus on directly connecting with our inner guidance. We achieve this by creating quiet time to listen within and stop being distracted by the outside world.

What expedites this process is having great compassion, grace, forgiveness for yourself and a sense of humor for not understanding the details of your incarnation.

As we become more present and a witness to ego thoughts, feelings, and behaviors, we begin to make other choices that shift our thinking to be more aligned with God's Truth.

There is only One mind. We believe that our thoughts shift us away from God, but that is part of the illusion. We are only lost in thought like daydreaming. We are unchangeable as Divine Consciousness.

We need to learn how to stay present as much as we can as we go out and interact with the world at large. We came here with a specific purpose, a Divine role, a script to follow. When we are present to the inner guidance everything flows easily.

## INTUITION

*What's amazing is that God is leading your life so there is no pressure to feel that you are living your life on your own. Your willingness to participate as a co-creator, listen, receive, and stay present is all that it takes to allow your intuition to guide you. Staying connected to your inner guidance makes your life so much easier and joyful.*

Everything we could ever need has already been given to us through God. It is our Divine gift as Creator. The ego's resistance and reluctance to accept and believe this Knowledge/Divine Truth, makes the work of staying present a life-long journey. The reluctance to believe and accept God's gift results in an internal tug of war (which is part of the illusion) between listening to ego or letting go and surrendering control to trust God. The ego is not an opponent…it is just a faulty thought system.

The ego wants to maintain the illusion that it has control over your 'will', yet there is only One Will. It is God's Will, and you are always in alignment with it regardless of what your ego-thoughts, feelings, senses, behaviors and experiences tell you.

*God's Will for you is to be happy, joyful, and peaceful and to Know that you are completely*

## THE NATURAL STATE OF BEING IS LOVE

*taken care of. He wants you to enjoy your life. You must be in an intimate relationship with Him to Know and believe His intentions.*

*Divine Consciousness is constantly shining more light (like a spotlight) onto situations that expose thoughts and beliefs that need to be shifted. This never stops. The more Divine Light that comes through you, the more faulty beliefs and thinking patterns become illuminated. People call the faulty beliefs, thoughts and actions darkness or a shadow side, however, there is no darkness, there is only Light. When you are present you can recognize yourself and all your external circumstances in the way that God perceives them as opposed to the way the ego interprets them.*

*You can look at darkness as a symptom of being Spiritually unconscious, ignorance: that is all that it is.*

As you begin to awaken, you may not even notice a shift in Consciousness is starting to take place. Even if you feel a change within you for only one brief instant a day, that connectedness will soon turn into a minute, then five minutes, and so on, and so on. Soon you will see and feel miracles happening as the veil of unconsciousness keeps lifting. Nothing on the outside is changing. The change is happening within you! ***You are perceiving differently and therefore, feeling differently.***

As you shift to a more expansive Consciousness you will begin to unravel all the programing that is a part of life's journey. It is not a race. There is no time limit. You must undertake your journey one step, one day at a time and do it with God because Divine support and Love heals everything.

> *Understand that there is no sin, no wrong or right, no good or evil, and no thoughts about not being good enough since your earthly existence is only a dream. Your innocence and purity have never changed.*

Each moment and each day are perfect whether you make choices to align with your ego thoughts or with God. You are used to beating yourself up and accomplishing your goals in accordance with a self-established timeline. This is not how the Divine process of unfolding and transforming works. You cannot force it, although your Ego will certainly try. Your conscious expands according to God's timeline and His plan for you.

## THE NATURAL STATE OF BEING IS LOVE

*You are exactly where you should be in a 'Divine timeline.'*

What is important is that you are consciously working on staying present as opposed to being stuck in the unconscious/trance of the illusion. Know at this very moment and every moment that you are doing the best you can. No judgment is warranted ever. You goal is to become an observer or witness rather than a judge of your Spiritual growth or lack there of.

The goal is to align with God who has created the Divine script or calling for you to follow. This is your awakening story. You have an essential role to fulfill within the illusion of your existence here on Earth.

You are like a student with an individual Divine curriculum. As you progress through your Spiritual journey you are learning the Truth of who you really are. As you deepen the inner connection to your Divinity you become aware of how you are being molded, polished, and made ready to unfold into your calling or purpose. Don't worry, this internal process is happening whether you are aware of it or not. Nevertheless, there is great joy in being awake to your unfolding. It is a masterful co-creation, and it all begins by opening your heart, going within, and receiving.

*God's Love transforms everything.
It is the secret code of life.*

INTUITION

## Journal Entry 5/30/17
## Meditation with Archangel Raphael

**Me:** I am trying to conceptualize the illusion and understand DNA. I am conceptualizing the Double Helix as possibly being a mixture of our Divinity & Humanity for each ladder. I am also trying to understand the power of intention within the illusion. Weird, I just felt a huge surge of heat, but what caused it? I think it is a lower vibration of energy.

**Raphael:** Very interesting you should notice that Deb. Sometimes your ego chimes in with fear and that creates a feeling of heat. Could it be that you were a little fearful of what I might say?

**Me:** Yes, Raphael, it could very well be because I had not met you before. I called you in because I heard my friends speak about you and thought you could be helpful to me as well.

**Raphael:** *There is no entity, Spirit or Angel that will create that feeling. Only your fear creates that sensation in you.*

All the lower vibration is from fear. Fear is the basis of it. Fear is what creates all the other negative feelings, and vibrations.

**Me:** That makes sense!

**Raphael:** Your ego is always active, hyper-vigilant, and fearful, so it can happen in an instant.

**Me:** I see how quickly that sensation of heat can come on. It's interesting that I notice the heat before I notice the fear within.

**Raphael:** Good, so now let's move on to conceptualizing the illusion. I noticed you were thinking that the Earth experience is like everyone having their own movie.

**Me:** Yes.

**Raphael:** That is an excellent way to understand incarnation. Each person has his or her own fantasy, a dream experience. It is their unique creative way to experience human life. So, Debbie, they are the stars of their own movie, and they can do and believe whatever they want, and Source is there to help them with it. Let us not perceive things as right or wrong. We don't judge others. It's their movie. If we do not like someone's movie, it's okay.

We do not have to like it. It is much like you not liking some T.V. programs Brian watches such as, Thrones or Sci-Fi. Look at it as a flavor of ice cream that you do not care for. It does not mean it is wrong. Each person is playing a role and you do not know what that role truly is. It could be just to add contrast to the way you think, adding color and contrast to your movie. It then gives you the opportunity to choose what you prefer. If the contrast was not there, you would not experience variety and be able to learn how to make decisions. So, nothing is wrong. Do you understand, Debbie?

**Me:** Yes.

**Raphael:** You have daily experiences with these opportunities. You decide: "I don't really believe or cater to that idea or behavior". This gave you more clarity about what you do believe or like.

**Me:** Yes, I see what you are saying.

**Raphael:** Now the illusion. *It is all an illusion. It allows each person to be the star of his or her own movie.* It is all for Soul growth, their expansion of Consciousness. Remember we are Souls experiencing different levels of conscious awareness and each one of us is learning different lessons at their own pace as part of the illusion.

## THE NATURAL STATE OF BEING IS LOVE

**Me:** I still don't understand how I could be told things by Jesus, God or the Angels and other people say that Spirit has told them something completely different, or the opposite of what I am hearing.

**Raphael:** I know that is hard to understand and there is no easy way for me to explain this to you other than Spirit is trying to help fulfill that person's growth within the context of what they have chosen, and that person could be at different stages of growth than you are. Remember, it is all an illusion. It is just a creative experience.

**Me:** Why does truth matter to me so much then?

**Raphael:** Because your life has been filled with so much that is untrue. But you already know Truth in your heart. You are very connected to your Soul's Truth of Love and Joy. You do not have to defend or prove your Truth to anyone; you just stand in it. It is your ego wanting to judge that you are right and someone else is wrong. *We just want you to accept everyone for the beautiful Soul they are and honor them for taking on the experience of physical life, moving towards their 'agreement' as you call it, to awaken. This honor needs to be applied to you as well.*

**Me:** Okay, thank you.

## INTUITION

**Raphael:** Now, DNA. It is an illusion.

**Me:** Then why do we look certain ways?

**Raphael:** God's magic of the illusion. The DNA illusion is so very powerful, you do not have to understand how it works, nor can you.

**Me:** What is your role with me, Raphael?

**Raphael:** To help you see life in a more expanded way, to remove the edge of seriousness from you and to help you stay in a state of Love with all because that is your True nature. *You do not have to view things as good or bad anymore. You must learn not to sit in judgment of people, yourself, experiences, or situations, because you truly do not understand the whole picture.* Take Brian, I know you are working hard on projecting joy for him and the both of you. I know it has been stressful arguing about money so often. *It is good to keep projecting happiness, but he is on his own journey and where he is, is perfect…both for you and for him.*

**Me:** I realize he is playing an amazing role in my growth, far more than I can even understand. So, should I not be envisioning us happy?

## THE NATURAL STATE OF BEING IS LOVE

**Raphael:** Yes, but take the pressure off because it will happen when the timing is right. You keep being your happy and joyful self. Do not make this about scarcity of money. *The lesson for you is to understand that you must be happy with things as they are now.* Visualize having money in a vault. A time will come where the vault is opened, and more money will flow to you.

**Me:** I see. I like looking at it that way. I guess this is just part of the flow of everything. The more I let go of controlling everything, needing, and wanting to make things go my way, the more the flow of receiving increases...allowing for much more abundance in so many ways.

**Raphael:** Enjoy the leading up to every moment of fulfillment, for your dreams are fulfilled. It is already done. Remember, the future is also the "NOW".

**Me:** Thank you, Raphael. I appreciate your help and Wisdom with this. It takes away the seriousness when I realize that I don't have to judge right or wrong, especially towards myself. I just need to try to go with the flow. Why do I keep seeing boats and hearing people say that boats are a financial drain? (at the time we lived on a canal)

**Raphael:** It is what people keep giving power to, so it keeps reinforcing it. You do not have to think that way. This is the power of intention working at its finest. The more you give power to something, the more it manifests. Everything is working beautifully.

## Journal Entry 9/12/18
## With God

**Me:** How do I become neutral so that I am only in a state of Love and acceptance? Or in a state of joy so that other things feel neutral to me? I believe that if you are in a state of Love, 'of being', it neutralizes all energy and balances it. Some people say God, that you can't or shouldn't be neutral, you need to take a stance or choose.

**God:** You are not defining neutrality correctly. A state of Love is not being neutral.

## THE NATURAL STATE OF BEING IS LOVE

**Me:** I was more concerned with not judging things as wrong or right, like I don't have an opinion either way. I can only do that from a state of Love and acceptance, but it does not mean I don't have my own beliefs or preferences. I guess that is where discernment comes in. Thank you, God. I understand this now, "a state of Love is not being neutral".

Journal entry 9/18/18 With God

**Me:** God, please help me understand and have clarity about anger, hate, sadness, jealousy, etc. Is this part of your nature?

**God:** I know this is difficult, Debbie. I taught you that for this human dream experience everything is vibration, as energy, and that energy varies from dense to light. The feelings you are asking about are different feels of vibration that have been named. I do not have anger or hate. You know clearly that My energy is pure Love and vibrates at the highest frequency. However, as a human or in the dream, you have the illusion of unbalanced energy or unbalanced vibration, so it feels like negative emotions. I don't have feelings. I AM Love and Joy, which are states of being and different than a feeling. The human dream experience is the only place where energy feels unbalanced which is Divinely purposeful. Truly, no one is ever out of balance because I keep everything in balance. There is nothing being done without Me. When someone appears to be doing something hateful, they are just in their learning process. Remember, this is all a dream, so no one is getting hurt.

THE NATURAL STATE OF BEING IS LOVE

Journal Entry 7/7/20
Meditation with God

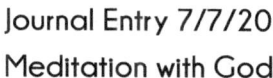

**Deb:** I Am the dreamer. I Am the creation of the dreamer. I Am playing the character in this creation. God is Consciousness – infinite and eternal creation/imagination. I Am One with God. I Am God. I am creation and the Creator. I think I understand more. I have chosen my parents and my story since I Am One with you. Jesus said this illusion was created for us.

**God:** Yes, Debbie, the story has been written just for you.

**Deb:** I wrote the story but don't remember writing the story or dream? So, I am the narrator and everything else I think I am experiencing within myself?

**God:** Yes, my love.

**Deb:** Right now, at this moment, when I am hearing you speak to me as Jesus or you God, I am just hearing my own self?

**God:** Yes, because there is only One.

**Deb:** I guess this Wisdom comes in stages. I understood at first that we were together, that you were with me. Second, would be that we co-create together. Third, that we are One in the same.

## Chapter Five

YOUR INTUITION IS ALWAYS ACCESSIBLE

*Belief in anything else other than Divine Consciousness is an illusion. Everything you see and experience in the physical world is merely a reflection of your human consciousness that encompasses the entire deception of duality.*

Have you ever had a 'gut' sense about something and recognized that it is a signal from your intuition? Maybe we have heard the soft whisper within not understanding that it is the voice of our intuition. I have questioned my own intuition many times and not followed through with what my intuition was telling me. This was due to a lack of confidence and trust in my own Knowingness. I relied on others to help me understand or tell me what I should be doing or feeling. This certainly gives power to other people to alter our reality.

This is one of the ways we create adaptations to our persona in a desperate effort to try to fit in with everyone else's expectations. It is similar to acculturation. We take on the faulty beliefs and ideas of society, culture, religion, and family rather than having confidence in our own Truth. Can you see how this gets in the way of hearing and trusting your own Divine authority?

At other times I have felt an energy within me that pushes me to follow a certain path or directs me to something I am meant to do. At times, the energy would be so strong that I simply followed its directive as if something within was moving me like a chessman on a chessboard. I didn't realize that what I was experiencing on a physical level was really my intuition guiding me. This is how God moves through you and it is happening all the time.

I would notice myself doing things, like preparing for some change or an event. It was as though an internal energy was moving me to carry out a task or action. I knew instinctively that a big change was coming without knowing what was going to occur.

I was not present enough to understand that my intuition was guiding and preparing me for something new. I now understand how powerful and important it is to be present and consciously connected to the Source of my inner Wisdom. God guides you through an intimate relationship and one of those ways is through your intuition.

God is quietly leading you all day long helping you to stay balanced and centered in Love although you never moved out of that state of being, you just believe that you did. It is extremely reassuring to know that you have this inner guidance available to help you know what is best for you in any situation.

Your guidance is also there to help you let go of things that no longer serve you, such as worry, fear or old victim stories. It teaches you forgiveness for yourself and others. This unconditional Love brings you peace, calmness, and a wonderful sense of reassurance.

God has created this amazing mirror for us to see and understand the internal dynamics of our Consciousness. The external world is a metaphorical mirror of the unlimited nature of Consciousness as imagination. As we awaken, we get to see our Divine nature and its creation.

We also get to witness the complexity of the ego and SPEC through people and situations we experience, all of which creates the appearance of separation between yourself, others, nature, and God. Through the awakening process we can clear the faulty belief of separation and stay ever more focused on our Divine nature and relationship. God helps us do this as He expands our Consciousness.

So how do we access our intuition, our inner guidance? If you ask, God will reveal Himself to you when you are

# INTUITION

in a state of peace and tranquility. You can achieve this stillness through deep breathing exercises or meditation and doing the best you can to empty your mind of its incessant mental mind-chatter. That being said, I have also heard God speaking to me when I was under great duress.

A good practice is to be still and quiet, take some deep breaths, be calm, and ask yourself for an answer to whatever situation you are working on. Or you can simply ask "Spirit, I understand you are within me, what would you like to share with me today?" It takes time to hear, Know, and recognize the soft ***inner feeling or voice*** that guides you.

> *What's important is that you can hear the voice of God, your intuition, in your very own voice.*

God reveals Himself at any moment. He speaks to you all day long. Being quiet and still just makes it easier to hear, feel and/or **Know** the loving Wisdom that is being shared with you.

The more you practice stillness and then actually follow through with what you have heard or felt, the more you'll develop a trust and confidence that you have guidance to know what is best for you. It takes time and practice to trust your voice because you are so used to listening to the ego. This is also the reason that self-love needs to be practiced. You have taken to heart hurtful things that you have heard from the ego thought system and which have negatively influenced the way you treat others and yourself.

I hear God as my own voice and as a male voice. I also hear through my heart. I Know when I am being spoken to. Your intuitive voice does not only come to you when you are in a meditative state. As mentioned before, sometimes you will hear the voice of guidance when you are in an emergency, when seconds matter. In these cases, you are typically in a state of shock or not knowing what to do which creates an opening for guidance to be heard.

Following your intuition isn't always going to be easy. At first it can be difficult to discern whether you are listening to God, or the ego thought system. Ego is very cunning. It will try to make you believe that its voice is the voice of God. The distinction is that God's voice creates peace within you; ego's voice does not.

That is not to say, that your guidance will never ask you to do things that won't push you out of your smallness, your comfort zone. It can be a bit scary when you are being asked to move out of your comfort zone.

When that occurs, you are forced to choose whether you want to push through your fears or give in to them. Sometimes you'll find the courage to push through. Sometimes your courage will fail you. It takes time, but if you keep getting the same message, eventually you will need to take a leap of faith and follow through if you are going to grow. This is how you learn to trust your intuition.

At times, you'll be able to recognize your intuition in hindsight. You'll see that you missed an opportunity because you resisted following your intuition. Yet, while you may have missed an opportunity this time around, it becomes a part of your learning process and you'll be more adept at recognizing your intuition and trusting your inner guidance in the future. You will always have other chances.

Your guidance is always with you and Knows what is best and loving for you. Ego is always trying to negate what your intuition is telling you. Ego fears everything and is only trying to protect you. It doesn't understand that you are always safe and unconditionally Loved. Ego does not understand that it is not real itself or that life is an illusion, a dream. Ego will resist what your intuition is telling you. At times you'll feel as though you are locked in a power struggle for control of you. This is an illusory battle, and one must not feed into it.

Let's consider resistance versus surrender for a moment. Many of us are resistant to practically everything, even if it's for our own good. Unconsciously, we allow our resistance to control our life. We are just like that rebellious little child that doesn't want to be controlled by its parents, or by authority figures. We resist our intuition, the voice of God because we believe in separation. We resist doing what is best for our self because we understand neither God's goodness nor our own inherent goodness.

The resistance is part of the constant undercurrent of Soul Print Energy running in the background of our mind. It is filled with fears, judgments, memories, and misbeliefs that keeps cycling like a tape recorder. This undermines our peace, strips away our confidence and creates anxiety and depression. As we react to the stress, we unwittingly project external situations that put us in a constant state of dis-ease.

This creates a recurring sense that something is wrong with you or that your life is doomed to failure, which is of course completely false. Jesus told me that it is really very easy to believe God's Truth and let go of the stories that are founded in SPEC. You just need to make a choice of which voice you are going to listen to… the voice of ego or the voice of God.

Overcoming the belief in separation is a process that takes time. You do not realize the subtle power of this 24/7 fear inducing thought energy as it constantly fills you with anxiety.

This gives us the impression that we have lost control. Typically, we respond by becoming ever more controlling of everyone and everything around us in a vain effort to establish some sense of stability and balance in our life. Many times, this overly controlling attitude takes the form of rebellion. When we are rebellious and controlling it is because we don't understand how Divinely Loved, guided, and protected we are. This happens when we are living unconsciously and have had traumatic experiences.

This 'rebellion,' stems from our not wanting to relinquish control to God. We think that if we relinquish control to God, we become vulnerable. What could be further from the Truth? Even though we may be in the midst of our awakening we may have not yet developed the capacity to consistently trust our self and God.

In the series "A Divinely Ordered Life." I wrote extensively about my own rebellion. I still experience resistance and rebellion to this day, but to a much lesser degree than before. There is nothing inherently wrong with rebellion and resistance. These behaviors are sometimes necessary. They are common and normal adaptations as we keep taking baby steps in our effort to surrender control to God.

When we are caught up in the illusion, we believe we have our own will rather than the Truth that we share One Will with God. The goal of this journey is getting into conscious alignment with God's Will which is for you to be happy.

We will resist and rebel at times throughout our journey and it will impede our ability to listen to our intuition. Of course, it is the ego that is orchestrating this resistance, going about its self-imposed job of 'protecting' us. Unfortunately, the ego is incapable of understanding that we don't need protection from our intuition. Many times, it is a wounded part of us interfering because we have not healed past trauma yet.

Letting go/surrendering control is a lifelong process. The goal is to gradually surrender the illusion of control throughout the journey and allow God to bring you the next experience in joy. Different situations will occur each day that will offer opportunities to acknowledge that there are very few things in life over which we have any appreciable amount of control. We can always plan and prepare for a given situation but that doesn't mean that we can control the eventual outcome.

*The only control we truly have is in how we choose to perceive and respond to things.*

These daily opportunities often involve the little frustrations and fears of life, painful relationships, work stress, finances, death, illness, or medical conditions. If you think about it there are probably a myriad of other circumstances in your life that make you feel that life is hard and unmanageable. You can feel like you have lost control. When you are constantly grappling with the perception that things should not be as they are, it creates anxiety and frustration. Resistance is a doorway to a journey of learning how to accept, allow and align. The more we can trust God the more we can allow Him to take the lead.

Pain, whether emotional, physical, or Spiritual is a sign that you are being confronted with an opportunity to let go of the false sense of control and have faith in God's goodness.

> *Associating or identifying with the body is what makes you feel pain. Pain is projected onto the body from the mind. I want you to stop associating or identifying with your body yet take care of it.*
> —Jesus—

You are being given the chance to take a long, hard, honest look at your pain and ask your intuition what the cause of the pain is. Typically, it is a faulty perception or belief that needs to be corrected or an experience that needs to be processed and healed.

As an example, you might have a deep-seated belief that you are a victim and will always suffer. This is perhaps one of the most common faulty beliefs. It comes from trauma, SPEC, family, cultural, religious, and societal programing. Your mind is creating external projections, stories that give you a mirror in which you can see a reflection of your inner thoughts and beliefs.

Situations will constantly arise that confirm your faulty belief system until you dive deep into the source of the pain. Many times, physical conditions come from holding onto anger, blame, guilt, shame, or hatred. It is energy that gets stuck in your body. Holding onto that pain is like drinking poison. As you keep allowing God to guide you, your perceptions will shift, and your Consciousness expand. Your pain will dissipate as your perception of experiences start to shift. This allows healing to flow in.

By allowing God to guide you as you seek the answers to all your pain, you are surrendering control. As you surrender control you are more willing to perceive and anchor your life through Divine Truth rather than experiences and a faulty belief system. Living in God's Truth, your new belief system can become: 'I can expect a life of joy, ease and well-being.' Your life will shift and become much more enjoyable when you think and believe Divine thoughts.

Surrendering and accepting life's circumstances rather than resisting them, puts us in a position to open ourselves up to allow and receive great Wisdom. We become open to Divine Love that wants to comfort and teach us. This is how we expand our Consciousness and grow through Divine Truth.

When we allow ourselves to be wrapped in the Loving arms of God, He teaches us to shift our perspectives and understanding away from our old and faulty belief system. Old thinking, beliefs, feelings, behavioral patterns, points of view and fears limit us and need to be re-evaluated. We are in the process of replacing everything we believed to be true because it is false. We are all like the 'Prodigal Son' returning Home. We are learning that, in Truth, we are Divine, a limitless being that is Holy, innocent, and loved beyond comprehension.

Take out a piece of paper and list the number of times that resistance or rebellion has had a negative impact in your life. Can you see how resistance or rebellion has shaped many of your life experiences? Is it playing a role in creating time for introspection? Can you find a reoccurring pattern? Write a little bit about how it might feel to relinquish control and surrender to a higher part of you that offers unconditional Love and only wants happiness and well-being for you.

## Chapter Six

### THE REBELLION OF THE EGO

*There is a great energetic force of rebellious thoughts that hinder us from wanting to accept and remember our Divine union.*

As we travel along our own individual paths, we often encounter feelings of rebelliousness, or we struggle through times where we are passive, apathetic, feel stuck and unable to advance. At times, it can feel as though we're constantly bouncing back and forth like a ping-pong ball between rebellion, commitment, and passivity. It can be tremendously frustrating. We see this often when trying to stick to a commitment to the gym, change a destructive habit or improve our diet. The trick is to recognize when we are caught up in this vicious cycle.

It's not always easy to recognize these thought or behavioral patterns because we are always flowing in and out of Divine Consciousness. Whenever we drop our guard and slide into unconsciousness, the ego immediately jumps back in and takes control. In fact, it is ego that uses its limitless ability to rationalize everything so softly and seamlessly that we gently drift back into a trance state believing what the ego is telling us. The ego can be sweet, passive, holier than thou or nasty, judgmental, and aggressive. It is an energetic trickster that makes us judge and doubt ourselves.

The ego thought system has easy readymade answers for everything. If we have a problem, it's not our fault says the ego. Someone or something else is the cause of our pain and suffering. It loves to rationalize and blame others or will turn on you and attack you for being at fault. Even when we are under the ego's sway, we may still believe that we're conscious, but we aren't. Many times, we are just stuck in a story and don't realize it. Let me give you an example.

During one of Barbara Di Angelis' workshops, I spoke up to say that for that past month I had been experiencing a deep-seated sense of resistance and rebelliousness toward my Higher Self and my Spiritual journey. As I worked with Barbara to understand the causes of my feelings, I began to realize that my belief in the system of pre-birth contracts was being challenged by the ego (see my book 'Are you ready to listen? -God'). I was angry to learn that this life's journey was already laid out in advance and that everything is in Divine order.

# THE REBELLION OF THE EGO

If our life is predetermined in some way and we are eternal beings, then there's really no place for an ego that feels the need to 'protect and control' us. It is always trying to control our responses to all the unpredictable pitfalls and challenges that life seemingly presents. Looking back on it now, I should have anticipated the ego's rebellion. All our fear, anger, disappointments, frustrations, etc. come from the ego's distorted perspectives. They fuel reactions that can end up in a misuse of our power.

I was caught up in believing the ego's perspective that made me feel as if I were a victim and being controlled. I felt like I was just a puppet, that I didn't really have free will, and that life is simply a farce or a kind of game. I looked at all of my and humanity's suffering and felt a deep sense of anger and frustration. I kept trying to rationalize how it could be that we are bound by a pre-birth agreement with God to experience so much suffering. It seemed so cruel.

This was a rather strange stance for me to take since I have only experienced God as faithful, beautiful, and Loving. He would not bring harm to me or to anyone else. In fact, God's Divine Love has transformed me and continues to transform me every day on a profound level. He is always shining Light on what needs to be shifted within. He also gives me the time and space I need to shift my perspective. This is Grace.

What I eventually realized is that I was even being fearfully influenced by various Spiritual articles I had read or things

I had heard because of ego's faulty perceptions. I needed to be more thoughtful or discerning about what I was allowing to influence me. I needed to discuss these things with my Spiritual guidance for clarity, which I eventually did.

It is the ego that does not trust God. Since we have unwittingly allowed our selves to be governed by the ego's faulty belief system, we do not have the faith or trust in God that we might think we do. As we go deeper into our relationship with God, we see our trust increase over time.

I realized what this all came down to was ego pride and not wanting to relinquish 'control.' I was still under the ego's influence. The faulty perception created a belief that the concept of entering into a pre-birth agreement with God was simply a manipulative game designed to give my Spirit a physical existence to experience life.

Believing this thought brought me terrible grief and anger because I was rationalizing through the 'oh-so-Holier-than-thou' Spiritual ego. I found, however, that by sharing my thoughts, feelings, and frustrations with the workshop group, I let those feelings of resistance and rebellion move through me.

This allowed me to let go of my belief that caused the ego-driven anger and fear. I was then able to make space for more Wisdom about the issue. I allowed the ego to put God in a very small box rather then understand the expansiveness of His nature. Neither I, nor you, can understand everything, especially the mystery of this existence. ***What I do know is that God did not create me or us to suffer.***

This is how we get stuck in the trance and make up drama when there is no truth to any of it. The Truth is that I AM blessed (as we all are) by a God who is good and that has given me the opportunity to live through creation and to serve by finding and living my True purpose in life, the one He/I chose for me to experience.

My rebellion was keeping me from seeing the Truth… that I needn't waste time and energy trying to understand God's intensions or why things are the way they are. We can never understand the mystery of life; that is why we have myths. The ego believed that I should be able to understand and make sense of everything. If that isn't pride and arrogance, I don't know what else to call it. The ego thinks it knows better then God!

I believe that we do indeed co-create the entire script for our life on Earth including our Spiritual return Home prior to our birth. We then embark on a fun experience where each of us is the main character in our movie. The movie is wholly designed and created with God just for us. We do not remember our script, which is purposeful and part of the forgetfulness.

Even though we/God wrote a perfect script for each of us, it is up to us how we choose to experience it. Our experience is based entirely on our perception of all things. We keep creating the same patterns of experiences based on our perceptions, our underlying beliefs about our self and how life works. These beliefs are founded in programing, our earlier experiences of life and the stories that we made up from those experiences. As a result, we each have our own subjective reality based on our own perceptions, programing, and patterns of beliefs.

*Remember that you are only pure Divine Consciousness. Your physical existence is an illusion, like a dream. It is important to understand that nothing is happening to you, everything is happening within you, in your mind.*

We need to turn within and ask God to teach us how to view situations correctly. We need help to Divinely perceive each experience. Only then will we be able to co-create the experience together with God in joy as our script and our transformation keeps unfolding. All our past, present, and future life experiences fit together in an expansive beautiful tapestry that entwines each of our individual stories with the ongoing story of the entire universe. It is absolutely fascinating!

Even when we turn within and ask for God's help it takes great humility, honesty, and faith to overcome our rebellion, our need to be right. We need to admit that we just don't know everything and simply trust that life is the way it is supposed to be without understanding why. Everything is in Divine order. It cannot be any other way. We cannot understand the expansiveness of God.

The anger and dismay of feeling like a puppet that I described above is just one example of many rebellious experiences so far on my journey. Working through ego's little rebellions takes time, patience, and compassion. It can be frustrating, but as you stay committed to your journey, you'll find these kinds of frustrating experiences will occur less and less. It is important to look at each one of these experiences as an opportunity to explore and experience yourself and to learn…rather than to judge your thoughts, beliefs, or behaviors as wrong or right. There is no wrong or right.

*All contrast is a gift to experience. It helps you accept all parts of your incarnated self, remember your Divine perfection, and to make Higher Heart centered choices.*

So, how do we recognize when we are starting to drift into a state of ego rebellion? Rebellion generally begins with feelings of anger, frustration or irritation as ego struggles to ignore our intuition. Ego always needs to be perfect and right. It needs to be in control. It is so very prideful. Pride is something that we all have experienced, and it rears its ugly head in many ways. Think about all the decisions we make that have their origins in pride.

Ego is our pride, and pride is our rebel. We self-discipline by not believing or feeding into ego thoughts. This is a challenging task. Our rebel acts like an immature, spoiled child who thinks it is right all the time. If allowed, it will take us off our Spiritual path because it doesn't want to give up control. It is like we left our five-year-old self in charge with its tantrums and immature beliefs of what will make us happy.

It doesn't want to give up its faulty belief in its 'free will' even if it goes against something that is good for us or for our true purpose in life. Since none of these aspects are 'bad or wrong,' our rebel self can do great things if used in the correct way. So can pride, if it is not coming from a place of narcissism or holding us back from doing the right thing.

Pride gets in your way, just like fear does. They are both doorways to walk through that help you to become more honest, self-aware, and clear. These aspects help you to see patterns of behavior and thinking within yourself that bring greater clarity to what is truly in alignment with what you want or believe. Even though we experience diverse thoughts and feelings, they are all part of the illusion. It is all contrast to help you choose what you want and believe. God's Will is the only Will and His and yours are the same and have always been in agreement.

Most often, if you just let go and hand the problem over to God rather than trying to figure everything out yourself, the answer comes through, or a shift occurs

## THE REBELLION OF THE EGO

within and externally. This minimizes getting frustrated with your self and with the process. I cannot count how many times I have said about experiences 'this shouldn't be.' This creates tremendous frustration. Our task is to learn how to allow, accept and align with Divine Truth.

When I worked with Dr. Barbara De'Angelis she discussed the difference between pride and humility. She described pride as "being concerned with who is right." We all want to think we are right. Humility is more concerned with "what is right." I had always thought that I was humble because I was always my own worst critic. For years I beat myself up, victimizing myself. That cycle of self-abuse lowered my self-esteem because I was stuck in a belief that I was 'not good enough.' I realize now that this was really my insecurity and self-rejection. This was not my humility. It had nothing to do with "what is right." Yet, it was all part of my process of learning about me. With the help of God, I was able to deconstruct faulty beliefs, versions, and stories I made up about myself. It is the perfect unfolding of me.

*Victim consciousness is an enslavement to fear that keeps you in bondage to the faulty perceptions of ego.*

*As you are processing your thoughts, beliefs, and feelings, allow yourself to be vulnerable without self-criticism. Self-criticism is persecution. Love yourself through life no matter what each moment brings.*

---

Journal Entry 4/17/16
with Jesus

---

**Me:** I am struggling to stay happy today. I falsely believe that 'happy' means upbeat, but I know it means to be peaceful. I also feel like crying. I am frustrated and I don't know why. Can you please help me, Jesus?

**Jesus:** Let's go for a walk. There is a lot of change going on in you and around you. I know it is confusing and overwhelming at times. It will settle down and you will feel much more at peace inside. Everything about you is changing. You are noticing and seeing that you need to spend more time by yourself to practice being peaceful because you are not around peaceful people. Your needs are changing. Do not be scared of these changes.

**Me:** I feel like I am too serious and don't know how to lighten up.

THE REBELLION OF THE EGO

**Jesus:** I know, but as you feel content and peaceful that will change. You are trying to understand things that do not make sense. Are you content right now as we are talking?

**Me:** Yes, although I feel like I keep getting pulled away from being content.

**Jesus:** That is right. The energetic undercurrents (thoughts) keep drawing you away from your center.

**Me:** What should I do?

**Jesus:** Just breathe and do what you already are. Stay here with me. Let's look at your book and see if we need to edit.

Journal entry 8/30/16
During Meditation with my Higher Self—
all stories and images are metaphors

# INTUITION

I see a cave with a waterfall and ledge in front of it. I am with my Higher Self and the warrior part of me. We walk through the waterfall into the cave. It is dark and eerie.

**Me:** Where are we? This is a dark awful place.

**H.S:** It is where the ego lives, in the dark. It does not see the waterfall or the sunlight. It cannot see it because it is not given the ability to. Only we can see it.

We walk back through the waterfall into the light. I felt sad for the ego that it had to live in the darkness and felt compassion for it. The unconsciousness makes sense now. The cave is a metaphor. It is a place we live when unconscious, however, we have the power to see through the duality with the Light and are able to move in and out of it. This is a metaphor describing how we waffle back and forth out of Consciousness.

THE REBELLION OF THE EGO

## Journal Entry 7/7/17
## With Jesus

**Me:** Jesus, I noticed I had a glimpse of seeing myself as a form of little pixels, as if I were a projected image from a movie projector, or hologram. I was wearing a red tank top and when I looked down at my shirt, it was pixilated!

**Jesus:** Isn't that cool? You are starting to actually see the illusion and how it is formed, but the human eye can't see this, you are seeing with your third eye. It is showing you the illusion, the projected image, like a projection on a screen…all the different light particles that make up you and color.

**Me:** That is fascinating! So, Jesus, is this everything?

**Jesus:** Yes, just projected onto this illusionary stage.

**Me:** It is like our Soul has an illusionary avatar, and that is us.

**Jesus:** Yes, that's a great way to describe it.

# INTUITION

**Me:** So, my Soul picked me as its avatar and picked my shape, color, etc. to experience and grow?

**Jesus:** Yes, but it is an illusion, like playing a role in a play.

**Me:** So, it is supposed to be fun learning?

**Jesus:** Yes, it can be fun if you realize that it's an illusion, it isn't real. It can be devastating if you think it's real.

**Me:** For a moment I thought I don't matter, because the body I see in the mirror and the mind I know and experience life with, does not really exist.

**Jesus:** Yes, that is correct.

**Me:** That understanding made me feel insignificant, sort of like a puppet that isn't real. I am a costume on a hanger in a wardrobe waiting to be used by an actor in a play. I have felt like this before when I first learned that life is basically a dream, and it is not real.

**Jesus:** Yes, you did, and it is okay, Debbie.

**Me:** I am not sure how to feel about that.

**Jesus:** Let's talk about it. Breathe. You are doing great. Your inner being, your Spirit, is still you, your Heart is still you, your Love is you, your Knowledge, your depth, and your "personality" or your energetic vibration is you. But your outer body is not.

**Me:** Why did that hit me in a strange way?

**Jesus:** It was your ego, realizing it is not alive, and all along it has believed that your body was the real you. You have been telling yourself you are not the body and that you do not have to carry illness anymore, that you want vibrant health. You want to remold your body, so it fits more with your new you, which is more of your Spirit. You have been recognizing there are no limitations on anything. You have been breaking through belief systems that would have you believe that you must comply with certain rules about how society says how things work or should be. Now, when I say taking away limitations, we are viewing this through a lens of Love, joy, and hope, not of power and control. That is why we are working on allowing God to bring you the next step as you keep removing the limiting beliefs you have about yourself and your world.

You don't have to go out into the world struggling and taking the bull by the horns because that is using force and power and control. You have done this your whole life in fear that if you didn't do this you would not get ahead. Your lesson is to know that all will be brought to you without the use of force. Force creates resistance energetically because it is coming from a place of fear or unbalanced energy. This, on a human level creates stress, anxiety, and illness. Your lesson is to learn you are Loved and can depend on that Love to bring you everything you truly desire. There needs to be no suffering or hardship to live the life of your dreams. At the right time it will come, and you have been guided all along. However, your energy was unbalanced and twisted up with fear, so the way you approached things was aggressively as if your dreams or desires would not happen otherwise. Your energy needs to be balanced with Love, not fear. You need to allow things to come to you, waiting patiently for the right time.

**Me:** Is this the Law of Attraction?

**Jesus:** Yes, it is, Debbie. Mostly it is about faith and trust and not using force, which is a fearful, frustrated, controlling, aggressive energy. It just pushes things farther away or makes everything a struggle. It is learning how to relax into calmness, faith, belief, and this allows you to have fun and feel secure. This is what breaks all the limitations of the beliefs that you have, such as you must

## THE REBELLION OF THE EGO

work hard to get ahead. You need to stop believing that something is wrong with you and that you are not where you are supposed to be.

It is very important to understand that it is your attitude that shifts things. You have worked so very hard over the years and poured amazing amounts of energy into everything you did which took a toll on you stress-wise. You always had an amazing attitude and integrity to do your best and be happy with whatever you were doing. If you weren't happy, you changed jobs or shifted your attitude to gratefulness. This is what helped keep moving you along as well as having a Divine vision for the future. Your vision included helping others and here we are again, starting a brand-new career full of vision, love, purpose, joy and wanting to help others in a great big way.

What is different now is that you have Me in your awareness, and we need to go about climbing this mountain to the vision differently. It is time to let go of control and show your faith and let us bring it to you in a much better and different way than you could have imagined it yourself. It is time to practice the lesson of peace and waiting with joyful anticipation and expectancy.

That means you need to keep balancing the energy within you since you have so much fire and feistiness to just go out there, grab at straws and take the bull by the horns. All of that comes out of your fear and feeling that you have do it alone. We need to balance your energy daily because it is still grounded in fear and makes you feel like you must take action immediately, by yourself, all accompanied with a great sense of urgency. That's just your ego and your will fighting to maintain their control over you. Your Soul Knows what is coming and the human part of you is so excited, but the strong undercurrent of some of those faulty beliefs are still acting out.

By practicing and believing what I teach you is how your Spirit matures and reaches higher levels of Consciousness. Your Spirit takes more control over your will and your humanity (ego). Your will and your ego will never completely disappear, but by daily balancing your energy you will be empowered to deal with the dichotomy within, attain more Light and Wisdom, and come into the Peace, Love, and Joy that is your Divine inheritance.

**Me:** Wow! This is a lot, Jesus, and on some level, I understand it all, but practicing it is another thing. I do practice, but I need much more self-discipline to remind myself daily. Really, you have brought everything to me, but I didn't understand that and approached everything I wanted with persistence and urgency. I believed I had to be the one to go get it and then hold onto it so tightly...

but there is no truth to that at all. I was afraid of losing what I gained. I understand all the energy you are talking about. I see it, Know it, and have felt it throughout my life. Now I am viewing things as a witness within myself when, before awaking, I was swimming in it with no awareness. I must tell you though; I am still struggling with the puppet perception. My feelings are sad and angry. Yet Knowing the Truth that I need not worry about anything, and that I do matter in a Divine way, should give me such freedom. I have mixed feelings and thoughts about this situation.

**Jesus:** This takes time, Debbie. Be kind to your ego that makes you believe that your body is everything. This doesn't mean that you should disregard your body. The journey is all about learning self-love while you are incarnated and how to treat yourself as a "whole being." The more your faith and trust in God grows and you let go of control, the freedom will come.

**Me:** I see.

**Jesus:** Appreciate what you have been given. Even in the illusion of life, the illusion of your body, you have been so blessed. There are many who have been given greater obstacles to overcome.

INTUITION

**Me:** Why does it appear that a little bit of Psoriasis is back when I believed it had been healed?

**Jesus:** You have been stressed over money, career, marriage, etc. and not dealing with it, and therefore, it's showing you what needs to be tended to, your emotions. It will go away for good and very soon. In fact, it is already terminated you just don't see it. Get rid of the undercurrent of struggle and suffering and watch it disappear again.

## Chapter Seven

### EXAMPLES OF RESISTANCE

*You are the center, heart, and Creator of everything you see around you. What are you projecting and perceiving?*

As I examine the role of resistance/rebellion in my own life, I am amazed to see the depth and complexity of the role it has played. What I found is that as you grow in Divine Consciousness your perspective expands and creates different levels of understanding. In the last chapter I described one level of awareness regarding the trait of rebellion. A deeper understanding is the awareness that all traits and aspects of your persona, including resistance/rebellion, are Divinely orchestrated and deemed perfect for your experience.

I previously mentioned that I experienced abuse growing up. My mother deferred to my father for discipline, and he used a very strict authoritarian style of parenting that included verbal abuse and physical discipline. This was not uncommon during the time in which I grew up. It is what my father experienced from his parents. There was a lack of Consciousness and compassion from my parents. This is part of the SPEC and programing that gets passed down from generation to generation.

I feared authority to a point, but gradually became more resistant and rebellious as time passed. I was a very strong-willed child (and still am) and had no qualms about standing up for myself, which many times brought me more pain and suffering.

What I recently learned is that the traits of resistance and rebellion are God given and are purposeful in how my story is meant to unfold, the story of me. I spent a lot of years believing that I was bad, willful and a problem. I now understand that I was simply acting as a mirror reflecting my parents' beliefs and behavior back to them. Through me, God was giving them an opportunity to expand their Consciousness and grow into a higher level of understanding. It may not make sense and at the time I did not understand it, but it was all being purposely and perfectly orchestrated.

A deeper understanding is that anything that I do gives me an opportunity to experience myself and learn from my thoughts, beliefs, and behaviors. If God oversees me then nothing is ever wrong. Jesus taught me that this experience is an illusion, a dream, and that I am really not doing harm and therefore, I do not have to carry any guilt, shame or blame others.

I know that this is a very difficult concept to internalize. This deeper understanding forced me to let go of my own victim story. It was time for this version of myself to transform. This took time and tremendous faith because I was so absorbed in emotional and body memories, especially from sexual abuse. I still needed to feel and process these terrible experiences to heal and let go of them. There are others who have suffered things far greater than I have. It takes great compassion for self and others to shift in Consciousness through acts of faith, trust, and Divine Wisdom.

We are being asked to believe Divine Truth over Earthly experiences and our physical senses. We are One with God and nothing bad can ever happen to us because we are eternal. All experiences become an opportunity to learn, to go higher in our perceptions and to expand our Consciousness.

As I grow in understanding and reliance on God's goodness, I realize that I do not have to use old coping skills or adaptations. They do not serve me anymore and little by little, step-by-step I let them go.

My resistance/rebellion played out in all my relationships. As an example, I had a pattern of asking my husband how I should handle something when I already had an idea of what I could or would do. Of course, he would give me an answer that wasn't in accord with what I was already thinking. I would then make the decision to do what I thought I should do in the first place.

My husband would ask me why I bothered asking him if I wasn't going to at least consider his advice. This would then trigger a belief within him that needed to be healed. Neither of us understood this at the time. Eventually I recognized that I was unwittingly setting him up as an authority figure (just like dad) over my choices so that I could rebel, feel powerful, and then follow through with my intuition even though I didn't trust it in the first place. I also recognized that by asking him what to do I was unconsciously creating an opportunity for contrast and to gain more clarity, which in turn gave me the confidence to go ahead with my original decision. Can you see how intimately God is moving in you and orchestrating everything?

I was able to recognize this same basic pattern of resistance/rebellion in my dealings with my children, my work supervisors, and even towards myself. As an act of rebellion, I would often not follow through with things that were good for me, such as exercise, healthy eating habits, cleaning the house or making time for myself. To create a sense of control within myself I was habitually late, withheld love from others and myself and I set up strong barriers to protect myself from getting hurt. I was

## EXAMPLES OF RESISTANCE

emotionally unavailable for intimacy and stayed safe in my own little world as a workaholic.

Over the years and even during my awakening I have picked on myself unmercifully for engaging in all these counterproductive behaviors. I was also critical of myself because I thought I was not integrating a Divine concept fast enough (Spiritual ego). I now know that judging myself is never warranted, as I am always exactly where I am supposed to be and that I Am Divine perfection in every moment. My Divine perfection or status never changes regardless of what I am or am not doing, saying, feeling, or thinking.

There have been times when I have resisted God and did not want to acknowledge His guidance. Thankfully, over time and with God's unconditional Love and help, and through my faith, trust, and sheer perseverance that resistance faded.

In the beginning when I didn't understand my awakening my ego was stronger. I was very resistant to listening to my Higher Self. Even now I can still be willful at times, although it happens less often. I would rebel by doing the opposite of what my guides tell me I should do. It's as though I simply covered my ears, so I did not have to listen. That has always been one of my standard patterns of rebellion throughout my life. I wouldn't listen to anyone because I didn't trust anyone, including myself.

## INTUITION

I have rebelled at times by refusing to accept God's Wisdom because I was trying to understand it intellectually; but you really can't do that. You must accept God's Wisdom through faith because it goes way beyond our limited understanding.

My resistance only lessened as I developed trust in Jesus and God. It was their unwavering Love, comfort and Spiritually re-parenting me with Divine Wisdom that healed and transformed me. It became more important to listen and trust Them rather than ego. I had to develop a relationship with my Creator before I could trust myself to listen to my intuition. At the time, I did not understand that it is all One and the same.

It takes time to accept and integrate Divine Truths. One that I struggled with is that I am not my physical body. We have a hard time believing that we are not a physical body because we can feel powerful in our body, we can feel pain, we become ill from time to time, and we watch ourselves age. Everyday we see something that tells us that we are a physical, flesh and blood being. It is easier to believe what the body 'tells' us rather than accepting God's Wisdom. We have learned to live life through our physical senses rather than Divine Truth.

The physical senses are purposeful in helping us create and experience life; it is all Divinely orchestrated. Although you may experience physical or emotional/mental diseases, they do not negate your Divine nature or

## EXAMPLES OF RESISTANCE

that you are eternal. The experience of any kind of dis-ease presents an opportunity to expand your Consciousness and to remember and become close to God again. You have your own individual journey, and your particular experiences are part of your Divine curriculum.

Another Divine concept that you grow to understand is that everything is energy. All our thoughts, feelings, beliefs, stories, our personality, and everything else that makes us who we are (or who we think we are) along with the external world are simply energetic projections, imagination, emanating from our creative Consciousness.

Everything we experience is created in our so-called mind. All energy, positive or negative, vibrates at different levels, different frequencies. A negative energy such as resistance creates its own specific energetic vibration. You can think of it as a low vibration, and you may experience it as feeling dense or heavy. Joy is a positive energy. It has a high vibration. It feels light and airy. Vibrating energy is what we feel, and it creates emotions in us.

As we grow in Consciousness our energetic vibrations come into greater harmony. There is less dissonance in our energetic projections. We shift the vibration of the energy that we are projecting through our perceptions and our internal dynamic; what is happening within us is based on our beliefs. We attract our own vibration in the form of an external situation. This is how the mirror works. If we project positive energy, we will attract positive situations and vice-versa…negative energy, negative outcomes. This is the Law of Attraction.

Most of us do not recognize all the faulty thoughts, fears and beliefs that hide in our unconscious mind. It is a Pandora's box. The energetic experience of those thoughts, fears and beliefs are purposeful. We must gain awareness of them before we can heal our belief in them. These energetic experiences also come alive in the external world to help us see them. The Spiritual awakening is a cleansing of all the programing. This process reprograms you to understand your Divine nature so that your beliefs are grounded in Divine Truth.

It is important that you understand that you are not totally creating this alone. God and you together as One have created this experience for you. You are the one who decides how to perceive it. It was meant to be fun.

Let's understand energy from a Divine standpoint. The more I resist something the more I experience resistance and frustration in my life. Whatever resistance I am creating within acts like a magnet that pulls back toward me at the same resistant energy. Energy follows thought and belief. It creates more internal and external conflict in a myriad of ways.

When both my husband and I are in resistance mode and trying to control everything and each other, it takes us both to another level of resistance that feels awful. The energy can escalate in a battle of verbal defense and blam-

## EXAMPLES OF RESISTANCE

ing. Eventually you will come to understand that you are only battling with yourself. No one else is there; you are arguing with yourself!

I could go on and on with endless examples of resistance and rebellion in my own life, but the important thing is that you become able to see how these energetic patterns are playing out in your own life.

Managing the resistance or any conflict inside of your self takes the discipline to compassionately witness your internal dynamic; this takes a willingness to do the hard work and invest the necessary time to learn how to perceive with a Divine Loving lens. God does the rest. This is a transition from learning how to master your outer world to learning how to master your inner world without self-judgement.

As you do this work you gradually start to take back the control that you unwittingly gave to the ego thought system by believing in it. You begin to operate from a foundation steeped in God's Truth rather than the false self you created out of fear and control. Life becomes more fun really when you realize it is what you came here to do. Spending time with God shifts your perspectives and helps you to interpret and respond compassionately to the complex web of your thoughts, feelings, beliefs, and situations. You are being taught intimately about self-love by Love itself.

As you go through this process of self-observation you learn that so many of your behaviors and thoughts are automatic and are rooted in past experiences and based on fears of the future. In fact, they are all energetic patterns that keep recycling over and over again. They just happen. There is almost no conscious thought process involved because we have habitually reacted to these projections and perceptions in the same way repeatedly.

When you are present and conscious you can catch these thoughts, feelings, beliefs, and behaviors as they occur, see them for what they are and choose to lovingly redirect your self. You need to step back from your automatic world and become present and a witness or observer to your conscious mind. Your intuition will guide you to the correct response. This is what I mean by 'discipline.' Self-discipline is an act of compassionate love. You don't need to keep re-traumatizing yourself.

In "A Divinely Ordered Life" book series, I talk about the outside world being a metaphor for all our internal dynamics. Rebellion and resistance are no different. They are a snapshot of the internal conflict between our Higher Self and the perceived ego. Your belief in the illusion of duality makes it appear as though there are two or more distinct parts of you, and they are always fighting for control. There is no duality; there is only One reality, and it is Divine.

Resistance and rebellion are part of the tug of war that goes on within our selves. This energy is palpable even though it is part of the illusion. We are constantly picking

## EXAMPLES OF RESISTANCE

on ourselves trying to live up to our image of who we think we need to be. This false image comes from SPEC that the ego uses to reinforce the belief that we are not 'good enough' as we are. Ego simply does not understand our Divine wholeness. As Consciousness you Know you are perfect and always have been.

You see this same dynamic on the world stage in all arenas including your personal life. What you see happening in the world is only a reflection of your own struggles and suffering that are going on within your conscious and unconscious mind.

As you awaken, you become much more aware of the mind chatter, its content, and the illusory war within. The task is to rise above and not get into a battle with the ego. It is energetically chaperoning you as a teacher of contrast for your journey. It presents you with opportunities to gain deeper Wisdom, to go higher in your choices and beliefs, to heal misbeliefs, to remember who you are. Do not give ego any power by arguing with it. Simply be aware of it, ignore it, and have grace and compassion for your self.

This illusionary battle with ego is just a phase of the Spiritual awakening that most of us go through until you believe higher Truths from God. Once you believe that you are One with God, most of the power struggle between self and ego defuses because you have come into alignment with Divine Truth and see your perfect innocence.

You realize you do not need to fight for control or mediate the internal conflicts anymore. You just need to be a dispassionate observer of the faulty thought system. It is very important for you to allow yourself to feel any feelings that might arise and then let the energy go. Keep choosing Truth and Love. There is no battle; there is only peace.

This Wisdom was shared with me over many years by God and Jesus. Today I am still learning how to trust my intuition although I am much better at it. It is still a work in progress. It has been difficult unwinding 64 years of conditioning and programing that taught me not to trust myself or anything else. With God's help, I continue to work on it everyday and can see amazing progress.

What is uncanny is that I am extremely intuitive and yet some part of me does not want to accept that. I found that hypocrisy lives in all of us because we view ourselves through two different lenses (Divine and ego) all the time. Eventually I learned to laugh at it all and stay for longer periods in my Divine Knowingness.

The good news is that the more you are in alignment (believing) with God's Truth, the more you recognize that all your transformation is taken care of for you. God is leading you, making the changes that transform you. It occurs year-to-year, day-to-day, moment-by-moment.

## EXAMPLES OF RESISTANCE

He takes over the task of mediation and if you are open and willing to listen, He always offers an immediate correction to your perception that leads you to a higher awareness. You notice the Divine corrections are automatic now. You do not even have to ask. You don't have to worry about micromanaging yourself anymore. If you are not hearing the guidance, then you ask within. It takes time and practice to be an open receiver.

God is moving within you all the time whether you are aware of it or not. He will take you higher into the Holy Self that you are. *Divine Love is always pulling you deeper into remembering your Oneness with and as Love itself.* You just need to keep letting go of control or trying to understand the puzzle, the mystery of you and life. God will bring Divine Wisdom to you when you are not dwelling on it and your mind is quiet.

The more time you stay present and open to God's Wisdom, the more you see that you are the perfect reflection of Him. There is a mutual Love and adoration for each other, and you now see and understand your Holy Self. This is a constant state of union and what is truly, Holy Communion. Your life becomes a metaphor for God's beautiful internal dynamic and not the unconscious duality of yours. Your mind is filled with joy and thanksgiving.

INTUITION

Journal Entry 11/7/17
With Jesus

**Me:** I have been thinking a lot about how I am experiencing life, people, situations, relationships, circumstances, and opportunities. I see there is a faulty belief, an undercurrent of thought focused on lack, or scarcity. I still see myself as not enough. I'm always feeling that I need to be more, better at this or that, greater than I am. I still focus on what other people can give me to make me more successful, yet at the same time, I am just enjoying being with others.

I love my family and friends, and writing, basically all that I do. I am witnessing myself through both sets of lenses, those of my Higher Self and my ego. This is happening simultaneously.

My ego is focused on my marriage needing to be different as if it is lacking in some way or not enough. It is actually perfect. Everything is perfect and in Divine order. It is just me believing that it is not perfect. Retelling old stories of problem relationships. I have no lack because

## EXAMPLES OF RESISTANCE

I have everything within me, but a story of lack is what I am creating, I need to create from abundance not from lack. I am viewing and experiencing my marriage or life through a distorted lens of lack, which is my faulty belief system, which then creates a continuous feeling and cycle of perceived lack. It's all a form of energetic recidivism, like a memory drawing me back to the energy of my Soul Print consciousness.

The same thing is happening with how I experience time. I feel that time is slipping away, and I have so much to do or want to do. There is no truth to that either. There is plenty of time. I don't lack time. I become overwhelmed and pressured by time when I focus on getting my career off the ground. I am creating lack there as well, experiencing time as lack. I am exactly where I am supposed to be, and everything is going right. There is such a strong resistance to stay in Divine Truth. Jesus, please help me understand this more.

**Jesus:** You are seeing very well, Debbie. This is a pivotal shift because it moves you from getting to giving. You already have everything. You have been given the ability to create everything, so you are not lacking anything. It is about giving, bringing forth more love, more creativity, more tools, and more information for people from your Divine fullness. You live, create, and give from a place of abundance within you. This is what creates the receiving that you are looking for. It is the reflection from the mirror image. What you are creating will be brought back to you. It must come from a feeling and belief of abundance versus lack. We operate from a place of giving because we already have everything. We create to share Love.

**Me:** I need to let this Wisdom settle in before I can gain more clarity and integrate it. I understood this principle, but I am now seeing it on a deeper level. My elevator just went up to another floor of Consciousness. It is believing how I want to be... "how can I help you, I have so much to give."

I can see this reflection in how I experience food too. I don't have to eat when I am not hungry. I don't have to overeat. I don't have to keep filling myself up because I am already full. I am abundant with everything because I AM everything. I have the capacity to create everything and anything. So, in seeing my career take off or climbing higher and higher in Consciousness, I need to feel like I have already accomplished those things. I am One with everything. I Am already where I long to be.

**Jesus:** Yes, you understand.

## EXAMPLES OF RESISTANCE

**Me:** I am full, abundant, affluent in every way possible and now it is set more in my belief system as Truth. This is the Truth! My ego has been telling me that I am still lacking, and I believe it…sticky, tricky ego and the veil of unconsciousness.

You are not saying much, Jesus.

**Jesus:** I don't need to. You are processing this very well. I am in awe watching you grow. I am so proud of you.

**Me:** Thank you, Jesus. I am full in the goodness of God. I need to stop seeing things as not good enough. It is a projection from within me. I am full within the Oneness, with myself and everything else. I am so full in my Love and Joy. I am fully happy with all aspects of myself and life, and this is True, I love my life. The projection from my ego that I am not enough, or lacking is so pervasive. I see it in how I am projecting it outwardly and then experiencing myself and my life circumstances. It has affected my marriage, family, finances, career, and relationships with friends. The projection is because I am not recognizing my own capability of who I am, my worth, my Divinity, or my own capacity to create or the freedom to perceive, view, feel, and experience everything without struggle. I keep trying to prove my worth or abilities by talking myself up and looking for reassurance from others. I just need to own my Divinity, believe it, and stop listening to my ego.

Journal Entry 1/19/18
Meditation with Jesus

Jesus and I are standing in the ocean. Both of us are ready to change from physical form to Light and blend our Lights together. This is another reoccurring meditation…becoming the Light together. This time my earthly father shows up and wants to join in as the Light. I hesitated. Parts of me did not want him to do this with us. It was interesting to see this arise in me since I felt total forgiveness for him. Those wounded parts of us never forget.

**Jesus:** Your father is the same as you and Me, Debbie. There is no difference between us.

## EXAMPLES OF RESISTANCE

**Me:** I spoke to my little selves and told them that it would be okay, and I proceeded. Jesus then asked me to bring my wonderful friend Susan into the Light with us. I did so without any hesitation. Jesus then asked that I bring my husband into the Light, and I felt hesitation again, worked through it and allowed it. So much resistance to include or see everything as the same energy as me! Then my mom joined us.

**Jesus:** They are all Consciousness just as you are. They are all Peace, Love, and Light. *Again, there is no separation and I do not want you to see them as the illusionary role they are playing on earth. You need to look past their egoic behaviors and earthly character. That is not their true identity, form or nature. You need to relate to them at their Highest. They are just God Consciousness, like We are.*

**Me:** This was an extremely peaceful exercise and not what I expected it to be. *So, this is a metaphor of integrating on a much higher level. I am not only integrating the sum parts of myself, but I am also integrating humanity (as the sum parts) to understand the Oneness of Consciousness. We are all the sum parts of the whole on a macro scale and that whole is God.*

**Jesus:** That was absolutely beautiful, Deb. I am astounded at your growth. You have understood this very well. You saw where you felt an aversion to not wanting to accept someone. You still wanted the separation due to judgment of feeling fearful and unsafe. But you worked through it, integrated, and saw there is only Peace and Love as the Light kept expanding with other people. I am so proud of you. We will continue to expand this practice so that you allow everyone to be part of you on a Spiritual level because there cannot be separation from God.

*Accept your brothers and sisters with an open heart and do not see them as their earthly role. See them as part of you, and that we are all God together.* We need all parts to come together. This is why I asked you to work on not seeing anyone as ill or dirty or bad or wrong. I do not want your fear of germs, illness, dirt, or wrongdoing to push you away from people or cause you to withdraw. *You need to accept everyone as the essence of God. This is the True integration of the sum parts.* Do you understand?

**Me:** I do. What an incredible lesson. Now I must work on practicing and believing that Truth and integrating it. Thank you, Jesus.

## Chapter Eight

TAMING THE WILL AND LEARNING
SELF-DISCIPLINE

*Embrace your enemy
for you are only seeing yourself.*

I remember the first time I became aware of the power of my 'will' as I started to heal wounded parts of my self. I encountered my five-year old self that was energetically filled with anxiety and fear. I believed I could not heal and integrate this part of me because the level of anxiety overwhelmed me. She was hyper, but all the hyperactivity was fear and anxiety from the energy and experiences from my childhood. My faulty perception was that this part of me was exhausting and annoying.

I have written extensively in "A Divinely Ordered Life" book series, about our Spiritual guides always being on hand to heal, Love and guide us. I brought

Jesus into several visual guided imagery meditations to help me understand my five-year old self. Many of us are disobedient or rebellious at these ages due to a need for control. This behavior can continue even into our adulthood. We can be outwardly disobedient or act in a covert or passive aggressive way. This disobedience is also acted out with God.

I would have spontaneous Divine visual movies pop up in my mind during meditation time or at random times during the day. In one particular visual I watched my five-year old self interacting with Jesus. They were sitting at a set of drums. She was sitting on his lap and playing the drums. Jesus was very loving to her, and she was very happy. She started to bang the drums with the drumsticks too hard and Jesus asked her to stop several times. She refused and kept banging harder. She was disobedient to Him. I was truly in awe of what I was seeing.

He took her hands and pulled them together as if she were in prayer. He held her hands together tightly but gently. After a few moments she was off his lap and sank to her knees and He kept holding her hands until the energy was transmuted into peace. She relinquished her will and surrendered to Him.

He then sat her on His lap and held her for days. She was peaceful and the hyperactivity, fear and anxiety disappeared. What Jesus was teaching me was how to discipline myself through Love. She just needed a calm-

## TAMING THE WILL AND LEARNING SELF-DISCIPLINE

ing, strong loving presence to hold her to make her feel safe and peaceful. I never knew how to soothe or comfort myself until Jesus taught me.

Most of us are not taught how to self-soothe or how to be loving or compassionate to our self. We don't understand that we can self-discipline without beating our self up with judgment or criticism, for that only causes shame and guilt. We need to learn how to discipline and self-soothe through unconditional Love and grace, to be gentle with ourselves.

Learning how to Love yourself, all of yourself, is a process. As I spent time with God and Jesus, I began to understand on a deeper level why I was resistant to interacting with my five-year old self. I misperceived her, (me) my inner child, as being needy, anxious, and overwhelming. All my self-judgments regarding these traits prevented me from liking or wanting to spend time with her. I had misconceptions about the different aspects of myself. At five years old, I believed that I was annoying, bad, and felt that no one wanted to listen to me or spend time with me. I believed that I couldn't make anyone happy. This self image came from how I thought my parents viewed me and treated me.

When I explored the origin of this belief further, I realized that I relied on others to define and discipline me. My father was very strict and controlling. My rebellious response was to act out and engage in self-sabotaging and self-destructive behavior. At certain periods of my life, I gave in to most whims and did whatever I wanted.

I had no idea how to nurture or soothe this rebellious part of me. I didn't know how to have compassion for my wounded inner child and all that she had experienced at a younger age. What I also came to understand was that I had absorbed the energy that permeated my home growing up…my mother and father's belief systems, anxiety, anger, unhealed trauma, and all their SPEC.

Through my teens and early adulthood, I smoked pot at times to avoid my feelings, anxiety, and the emptiness in my heart from life experiences. As I grew older, I disciplined myself very strictly to gain some degree of control over my behavior. I tried to be the good girl, the person that everyone expected me to be as well as the faulty image of what I thought I should be. If I felt overwhelmed by anxious or uncomfortable energy my unconscious response would be to go shopping and spend too much money or throw myself into my work until I was physically exhausted. I was overwhelmed and stressed out from all the busyness.

Even though this nervous/anxious energy was having a huge effect on my life, I didn't even realize that it was running through me. I didn't realize it because, for most of my life, I was numb to my feelings. I disregarded how I felt. The numbness was an ineffective coping skill to protect myself from feeling emotional pain and hurt.

## TAMING THE WILL AND LEARNING SELF-DISCIPLINE

Suppressing all this energy took a toll on me. When you are living life like a hamster running in a cage your body is releasing dangerous levels of chemicals such as Cortisol and Adrenaline. These chemicals are only supposed to be released during traumatic events. When you live life in a constant state of hectic busyness and stress these chemicals are released daily. You become addicted to the rush of energy without even realizing it. Living in an ongoing state of stress or survival mode creates chronic medical issues and increases anxiety.

I was in denial. Many times, people are diagnosed with bipolar disorder, anxiety, depression, or other mental health problems when the underlying causes are traumatic life experiences, SPEC, feeling unbalanced vibrational energy stemming from an unconscious belief that they are separate from God. These are patterns of painful stories and recycled faulty beliefs that have not been processed, resolved, and released.

When there is unresolved pain that produces so much energy inside of us, we can also become very impulsive. Feeling over-joyed can result in the same problem. If we are self-rejecting, we don't take the time to turn within and tune into the energy and our feelings. We just react to it or suppress it and want it to stop. This creates energetic resistance within.

Recognizing the energy that flows within us is critical in understanding how to transmute that energy and move it out: allow it, be present with it without judgment or resistance. Eventually it will transmute and dissipate. As an aside, deep breathing and relying on our intuition to guide us is very helpful in this clearing process. It's important to remember that feelings and thoughts are energy.

Suppressed energy and avoidance of our feelings can often be the cause of certain physical pain, compulsions, obsessions, and addictions. The obsessions, compulsions and addictive behaviors are ways for us to distract ourselves when we are overwhelmed by unbalanced energy, irrational fears and forgetting our Divine nature.

When we indulge in our obsessions, compulsions, or addictive behaviors we are simply trying to mask or numb the energy or run away from it. However, tuning into this energy provides a great opportunity for us to become present, experience ourselves fully, confront our fears and use it as a means for healing. When we are present the door opens to Divine Wisdom that helps us perceive and navigate our life journey differently. The energy will continue to follow us until we heal it.

It is our belief in a dual mind that creates all our issues. Many times, the overwhelming content of mental (thought) energy gets stuck in our body and causes us to experience physical pain. Have you ever experienced physical pain when you were feeling anxious, angry, depressed, grieving, overwhelmed or when you were unable to forgive yourself or others? I have realized that much of

## TAMING THE WILL AND LEARNING SELF-DISCIPLINE

my physical pain was coming from not speaking my truth, faulty beliefs, unresolved trauma, anger, self-hatred, and pressure that I put on myself due to believing I am not enough. When I recognized this, it became the perfect opportunity to see where forgiveness is needed so healing can take place.

*Forgiveness is how we let go. It dissolves the grief and judgement of what should have or could have been. It creates space for acceptance of what is or was, or what you thought was to be. Acceptance makes room for freedom; it allows you to flow in Divine peace.*

*We are really doing the best we can. We simply forgot who we are, God's Truth and His Divine Love.*

You can only begin to balance or release the internal energy when you confront its root cause and learn how to be compassionate and loving toward your self. You do this by being quiet and ask within what you are feeling and why. Ask also to be shown what needs to be healed.

When I first awakened all the numbness was wearing off and all my suppressed feelings started to arise all at once. I had no idea what I was feeling or why I was feeling it. I was feeling everything. I was overwhelmed and could not make sense of it. I was not used to feeling so much emotional energy, let alone all at once. Upon awakening many people feel like they are losing their mind or that they want to crawl out of their skin. Once that stage clears you can revel in feeling your own vibration of Love, a tingling sensation that pulses through your body. You feel alive and it feels great when you experience it.

As you learn to become more self-aware, you may find that you are feeling energy that is not real or current. It could be just a memory of an uncomfortable moment in your past. Many times, your inner child is asking for attention to heal past experiences, and this is the only way to get your attention. Ask your guidance for help in understanding.

You must take the time to peek inside your self and start tuning into your intuition to understand what is happening within. To begin the healing process, you need to become aware of the energy that is brewing inside you that has been created by your thoughts, experiences, and perceptions.

When you ask your guidance for help you are opening the door to learn that you are always in balance because God is always in balance. That never changes. You get caught up in the illusion and delusional stories and feel unbalanced by the energy of your thoughts, experiences, and beliefs. God is the only One who can heal you with unconditional Love and teach you through Divine Truth how to live a loving, happy, and peaceful life.

## TAMING THE WILL AND LEARNING SELF-DISCIPLINE

God has taught me that everything I am feeling is within me not in other people. Within the illusion you believe that you are feeling other people's energy or emotions. In Truth, you are only feeling the complexities of yourself, past and present...the dynamics of your conscious and unconscious world projected outwardly.

When you engage in deep introspective work, you sometimes find that you dislike different aspects of your self. As I looked within and engaged with different aspects (ages) of myself, I realized that I had a lot of self-loathing and rejection that I had not recognized before. It was God that taught me to accept all aspects of myself and Love myself fully and wholly without judgment. To see myself as Divine, whole, and innocent.

When we dislike something that is an integral part of us, we often disregard it and have no compassion for it. We pass judgment on aspects as positive or negative, good or bad, right or wrong, but there is no Truth in it. The ego judges the aspects based upon its faulty belief system. God teaches us that all aspects are perfect. He created each one of us perfectly.

Growing up I felt devalued and disregarded based upon experiences I had with my family. The ego created a faulty self-concept and image out of my feelings, faulty beliefs, and limited understanding. As a result, I thought of myself as devalued and treated myself with disregard.

## INTUITION

You can't heal your wounded aspects until you can find Love, forgiveness, and compassion for your self. The idea behind healing the faulty beliefs is to stop believing in suffering, grief and misery and accept and **BELIEVE** God's Truth and your Divine identity. It is one thing to accept God's Truth intellectually, but it is another thing to **BELIEVE** it. You must believe it in your heart of hearts. This is a process and where faith comes in. **FAITH IS THE BRIDGE TO BELIEF.** As you learn to live in Divine Light and Truth you are led to a path of joy, Love, passion, purpose, and peace.

We often treat our selves and others with a lack of compassion and regard, if that is what we have experienced from others. Sometimes we treat others better than ourselves. We place them on a pedestal, because we do not understand the grandness or Oneness of who we are. We are all equal because we are all One with God. There is no separation within us or amongst us. There are no battles within or without other than what we create in our mind.

The taming, disciplining, and accepting of our self with all of our diversity, must be done with regard, compassion, and Love. An unlimited capacity for Love, compassion, forgiveness, and regard resides within our heart. That capacity is never lost, no matter how deeply we think we've buried it. Our heart is the same as Divine Love.

## TAMING THE WILL AND LEARNING SELF-DISCIPLINE

> *Our Creator is always ready and waiting to show us how to open our hearts, uncover our Love, and nurture us back into the loving sovereign being we are.*

The ego knows nothing of Love, forgiveness, compassion, or regard; it never will. As we open our heart and mind to God, the lessons of compassion, Love, forgiveness, and grace can be learned and developed to apply towards our self and others. It took a very long time for me to accept and believe the unconditional Love that Jesus and God had for me. When I did, I was finally able to transfer it to all the aspects of myself and others. This is an ongoing lesson. Other people show up in my life and at times I need to call on Grace to help me through moments of judgement or withholding Love.

As Jesus quieted and redirected my five-year old self, she was not only soothed and Loved she was treated with compassion and grace for her actions and misbeliefs about herself and the world. As Jesus nurtured her, I was able to let go of the belief that no one liked me or that I needed to rebel or be disobedient to be heard. I was Divinely corrected about who I truly am...Divinely perfect just as I am. This is a good example of being Spiritually re-parented. This is what creates transformation. You are unlearning and relearning everything about you and this life.

## INTUITION

You can spend time with your wounded inner child and Spiritual guide through visual guided imagery. Practice loving him or her and seeing these aspects of yourself through God's eyes and not the ego's eyes. In fact, over time, we need to see everyone through the eyes of Grace, including the illusionary role of the ego. Invite your inner child and God to join you in your visual meditation, you will be amazed at what you learn. Always ask God to help you understand the Truth of what you heard from your inner child.

When you experience God, Love itself, you understand your perfection and there can be nothing that ever changes that. There is nothing on Earth that compares to God's Love, that's why I give it a capital L. It doesn't matter whether your guidance is Jesus, Angels, Buddha, the Light, the Universe, Source, Consciousness or loved ones who passed, they are all the voice and mind of God. Nothing else exists.

God wants to keep nurturing you to strip away the false self and to allow you to expand into your true being…to show you the blessing and miracle you truly are. This only happens when you spend as much time as you can being aware and conversing with God. This does not mean you aren't living life or not experiencing the illusion. You are simply more focused on the connection to God's Truth and less driven by the ego thought system. God will direct you always having your best interest at heart.

## TAMING THE WILL AND LEARNING SELF-DISCIPLINE

His beautiful Love lifts you out of the lies you believe about yourself and others. However, you have spent your entire life believing the illusion and lies, and because of that, it takes time to believe and trust in God's Truth.

You will continue to get sucked back into the trance. This is why connecting to your intuition is so important. You need to use your Divine Knowingness to override your thoughts and senses at those moments when you feel overwhelmed by SPEC and what you see in the world. Your intuition needs to become your default system instead of trying to figure everything out as you experience day-to-day life.

Our current default system is to perform and to act in certain ways so that others will like us. We do this because we do not believe we are perfect and enough. We have fine-tuned our behaviors, the way we dress or speak and scrutinize everything we say or do. We have not learned how to self-discipline the mind-chatter, our ego, our will, or how to rescue the wounded parts of us that are crying out for Love and healing.

We cannot force the ego voice or thoughts to stop. When we try to the resistance starts. I know first-hand. I did not want to hear ego thoughts, I thought they should just stop...but they don't. It is very important to allow the ego voice and just ignore it. We do not need to get frustrated when we experience both ego thoughts (mind chatter) and Divine thoughts simultaneously. It is just the illusion of duality that is the foundation of our earthly experience. ***Know and accept that both will always be present. It is your choice which to listen to.***

Please remember everything is in Divine order and created so that we can awaken and return Home. This journey is supposed to be fun! Once awakened your life takes on a whole new meaning. It is a miracle. You are a miracle and so are the wounded parts of you that are calling out for healing.

> *Our journey of transformation is to believe God's Truth and integrate Divine Wisdom. The miracle is that you can never lose your way. God is guiding your every step.*

---

### Journal entry 7/3/17
### Meditation with Jesus and John the Baptist

Jesus, John, and I are on a fishing boat out in the ocean somewhere. The waves are high, the boat is rolling around and I am trying to balance myself so I don't fall. John and I are watching Jesus release fish from a net in which they are entangled.

# TAMING THE WILL AND LEARNING SELF-DISCIPLINE

**Me:** I feel like those fish sometimes when I listen to ego thoughts and feel the pressure from my will. I wish I could break loose out of that tangled web.

**Jesus:** You can...and much of it is just deciding not to listen to it. You can choose either inner calm or turmoil.

**Me:** I forgot; it is my choice. I am the one that chooses tranquil seas. I keep getting pulled back into ego thoughts and stories and I forget. I need to be stronger and use self-discipline when my ego and my will interfere with my peace. I need to keep the seas calm. I keep forgetting that I need to decide and choose not to struggle or suffer. I understand this is the next phase in my Spiritual growth and staying present is of the upmost importance to accomplish this. I need to learn how to keep my foundation steady and stop relying on you to do it all the time, even though I know you are always there for me.

I mentally balance the water and the boat is calm, no more waves, although my ego wants to stir the water up again and I must breathe to move that voice or thought system out of the way. This is a constant practice.

# INTUITION

## Journal entry 9/13/18
## With God and Jesus

**Me:** God, I do not like the feeling of resistance in me. You are telling me to let go of a situation and a part of me does not want to give it up. I feel like I am losing my freedom if I let go of this situation. I want the resistance to let go of me rather than me letting go of a situation. It's crazy! I'm so frustrated with myself, and I want it to stop.

**God:** All the feelings are there for a reason and I love ALL of you Debbie, every thought, feeling and action. It is important to have loving compassion for yourself and embrace all aspects of you and all of your feelings. None of it is wrong.

**Me:** All these different feelings are what makes us feel alive. It creates what we think life is…drama within the illusion. I need to stop thinking that feeling this way is wrong or bad or problematic. The more I focus on wanting it to stop I create more resistance and frustration.

**God:** Embrace it all and find the gift in it.

## TAMING THE WILL AND LEARNING SELF-DISCIPLINE

**Me:** If I allow these feelings, they can give me clarity about what I truly believe.

**God:** Remember, Debbie, I have already given you complete freedom. People or situations do not give you freedom.

**Me:** The resistance is my will going against what you want me to do. I am acting out of the ego, SPEC and its faulty beliefs and fears. The ego wants to stay in control because it fears it will lose its power. It is like having wind chimes. Once the wind blows the tubes bang into each other, creating different tones and affecting how I feel by the sound they make. The vibration of this energy either feels pleasant or not pleasant. The whole symphony is neither wrong nor a problem. I just need to balance the noise with Love to become neutral or peaceful. Part of that is not judging the noise inside…just accepting it by bringing Love and compassion to myself. The noise, the chatter, is telling me a story and I decide what the truth is. I need to look at myself as one big energy-balancing system. There is no conflict or problem other than what I perceive. Your Love, God, conquers and balances all. Your Love and Truth smooth everything out in me.

**Jesus:** You need to look at the resistance as "Yippee…another chance to bring Love to myself and smooth out the tension, resistance, anger and irritability…transform it into mushy love, Debbie".

# INTUITION

## Journal Entry 4/24/22
### With Jesus - He is holding me and a family member.

**Me:** Jesus, I am having visions that are very upsetting. They keep coming in flashes especially when I am trying to sleep. I know they are coming from the ego trying to induce fear in me. I keep seeing a car accident and a broken piece of car window glass impaling someone I love. It is very disturbing. Please help me know how to handle this since I just keep saying 'stop' and it just keeps coming.

**Jesus:** Stop resisting the image. Let the glass go right through us, it is just energy and cannot hurt you. This is ego fear. Just let it pass through without judging or fearing it. All is well. It is just an energetic thought. It does not change anything. You are shattering all the old faulty beliefs and patterns. These images will stop because they no longer affect you.

**Me:** This understanding brings me peace, Jesus. I am looking at the glass as if it is just water, just vibrating energy. I don't know what I would do without you and your Love, comfort, and Wisdom.

## Chapter Nine

### DESTINATION INTUITION

*We all fly on Angel wings
even if we can't see them.*

If you use the visual guided imagery technique, make sure you bring your Spiritual guide into it with you. It will provide support as you work to heal your wounded inner child and clear out the unresolved hurts and beliefs that are blocking you from listening to your intuition. It also frees you up to experience more fun and joy in your life because you become more playful.

This does not mean that the thoughts or feelings of that hurt inner child are going to disappear. However, over time, the energy, thoughts, and feelings will dissipate, and you will be less triggered because you have stopped attaching to those faulty beliefs and experiences. You are healing from your old story.

## INTUITION

It is important to remember that what we are dealing with is only an energetic illusion. We are energetic beings. The memories, feelings, thoughts, etc. are recycled patterns of SPEC playing out unhealed fears and faulty beliefs. Eventually, we will be able to recognize when that hurt little inner child is filling us with fear energy, anger, and anxiety. Slowly but surely, we stop feeding into that energy and aren't overwhelmed by it like we used to be. We learn to allow the uncomfortable thoughts and feelings and meet them with presence, Love, and compassion. This essentially melts; it transforms the energy. Love is the only alchemy we ever need.

I like to ask within myself 'what is causing these feelings?' I typically get an answer quickly. It is very important to accept what you hear or feel rather than tell yourself you shouldn't feel that way. That only creates shame, anger, frustration, or guilt. This causes a pattern of resistance, and it is the way the Spiritual ego works. You have gained a lot of Spiritual Knowledge and the ego thinks it knows better than having to feel difficult feelings. It never wants to feel pain because it believes you can't handle it. The ego tries to have you bypass or transcend your humanity. Because you are awakened it feeds off beliefs that you are holier than thou and don't need to address your feelings.

For a long time, I was able to speak or describe my feelings but was not allowing myself to feel my feelings. This is counterproductive. All you need to do is observe, simply feel your feelings, bring Love, and compassion to yourself and let it go. I like to journal during these times. You will gain Divine insight as to what they were. At other times, I wasn't sure why I would start to cry and realized I just needed to move the energy through me.

It can take a lifetime to identify and remove all the unresolved faulty beliefs because we still cling to the belief that we need to be healed, even though God tells us we are Divine, whole, and perfect. I cannot tell you how many times God has reminded me that my experiences are just a story, yet I have taken them to heart in the deepest ways.

The energetic faulty belief system has such a tight grip on us. Choosing to believe and trust in God's Truth over the illusion comes by the way of faith and intimacy building with God. It all comes down to choosing. There is no pressure from God because there is no such thing as time.

The good news is that as you begin your inner work, you'll be able to recognize and access your intuition fairly quickly. As you continue to make progress, trust in your intuition will grow even though the ego's programming has not been overcome.

Your intuition holds all the creative plans for your life. It Knows your true purpose and what truly makes you happy. God wants you to connect with your creativity and allow it to surface. God wants you to learn it and revel in it. You were born to create!

## INTUITION

Your Creator has placed a treasure trove of Wisdom, gifts, talents, and Divine purpose within you. It is His Will and yours too, to consciously co-create this purpose. This requires that you develop a reciprocal communicative intimate relationship with God so you can be taught what those gifts are. The Divine plan for your life will unfold whether you are awake or not. However, it is such a joy to be awake within the experience. God also loves to surprise you and each one of those moments are such gifts and miracles.

It's critical that you take the time to give yourself this opportunity. Start by taking just a few minutes each day to be still, quiet or meditate and ask to be shown your gifts. Explore whatever images or thoughts come up. If you get an urge to try something different, a passion, or return to some creative endeavor that you have drifted away from, follow that urge.

We are used to suppressing, disregarding, or inventing reasons why we cannot engage in our creative or passionate pursuits or activities. We rationalize why we can't do these things. We make time and or money an excuse when they do not need to be. The root cause of our avoidance is usually guilt and a feeling of unworthiness. We forgot that we are unlimited beings. These are faulty limiting beliefs that betray a lack of trust that God will provide if asked.

Most of us don't know how to Love our self and give our self a life filled with peace, contentment, passion, and the purpose that we so much desire. The guilt and our avoidant behavior are the products of our ego and its irrational programing.

The ego keeps us busy doing things that don't inspire us. At times this avoidance is manifested as codependent behavior. We try to take care of everyone else and neglect taking care of ourselves. We need to begin the process of self-discipline of our ego thoughts so that we can allow our self to be creative and enjoy our lives. When I say discipline, it means ignoring limiting ego thoughts.

All it takes is not listening to negative or 'can't do' thinking and then gently moving yourself into the creative process that you desire. Remind yourself that you are an unlimited being and have the power to create anything you want. It is your Divine gift. This is true abundance.

We are responsible for our own happiness. Happiness is our natural state; it is our Divine nature. Yet so many of us never feel happy and don't know what would make us happy. Our happiness gets buried under our negative thoughts, traumas, worries and fears. You are the only one who can allow yourself to experience your own happiness and fullness because it is already within you.

Choose something you really would love to do, like a hobby, or going to the gym, taking a class in something that interests you or engaging in a creative project. Let your passion lead you. It can be anything. Put it on your calendar and make sure you follow through.

## INTUITION

Dismiss your ego if it objects. Do not give it energy. Do not argue with it. The ego is conditioned to make you feel guilty so that you don't indulge in things that you are passionate about. Do not let it make excuses for you. Do not attach to what it is saying. Be aware of the commentary in your mind and simply let it go. It is only the illusionary voice of a faulty limiting thought system that you have mistakenly allowed to govern your life thinking it is your true voice. The more you stay present, the more you will be better able to recognize the ego voice seeking to distract you.

You may find that you have trouble getting started at first but keep at it. Be patient and persist, but don't put pressure on yourself. Don't be too hard on your self if you miss opportunities to follow through. You will never run out of opportunities. Find the time to compassionately work on your goals each day of staying present.

Some days will be easier than others. Don't beat yourself up by thinking that you must see clear progress every day. Make sure you are not using an ego thought system to quantify what success is. Simply do your best each day and find a way to incorporate your passions into your daily or weekly routine. It is not always easy, so be flexible as life will try to interrupt your plans. It takes a true desire and willingness to follow through. Whatever happens is perfect; it is what it is. Accept the process as an opportunity to witness your thoughts, feelings, beliefs, and behaviors. You get to experience yourself in every moment.

Eventually, you will get to a stage in your awakening when you can let go of more and more control to a Divine flow. As you do this you will find that you can just follow the flow of energy within you and let it guide you. You allow Divine Love to create your day instead of you planning everything. It feels effortless, fun, and peaceful when you are in Divine intuitive flow.

Developing Spiritual muscles and staying in Divine Truth takes time. The more you realize that you are dealing with an illusion and that there is no real internal or external battle, the easier it will be to go with your intuitive flow.

Ask your guidance to help you figure out a routine that would be more loving to yourself. If you have days with different schedules, as I had, you can ask when the best time would be to do a particular activity. Once you are connected more with your intuition it will be easy to figure things out as they occur each day. Eventually you will be able to allow the day to flow as it wants to, because you believe and Know that God is good and guiding you all the time.

## Chapter Ten

WHY DO WE RESIST TAKING TIME
FOR WHAT WE NEED?

*My Heart is your heart,
what will you do with it?*

Even when we Know what we need, we often stall or delay doing what is right for us. It takes time to learn how to instinctively trust and follow our intuition. It takes time to learn that it's okay to be good to our self and not keep putting off what we need or what our intuition is nudging us to do.

As I sit here writing this book, I am aware that I need a break, to get a drink of water, go to the bathroom, or just get up and stretch; but I am postponing, pushing through, stalling. My husband is hard at work sitting across from me editing my books, and I hear his frustration. I say to him, "maybe it's time for a break, walk away, get a drink of water." He is my mirror, a projection of myself, yet it took a moment for me to see it.

It's amusing to me to see that I am not doing what I should do for my self, and now I'm projecting my needs onto my husband. The mirror is so fascinating. He does not move either, still typing away. After seeing the absurdity of all this, I finally decide to get up and follow my intuition. I would never have witnessed what I was doing had I not been present and in a state of peace.

All of us engage in these types of delaying, avoidant behaviors daily. Think about how many times you want to speak your feelings, but the fear of being truthful and how others might respond shuts you down. We can delay and avoid even when we are centered, present and peaceful because the ego is still actively working within.

The ego is very adaptable and employs a variety of different strategies depending on the situation. My ego likes me to keep my nose to the grindstone without coming up for air. It is the way I have approached work all my life. This is not a loving or balanced behavior.

There are a multitude of reasons why we delay or resist giving our self what we need. Most of those reasons relate back in some way or another to our belief system and societal programing. We must understand that it is not unusual to experience this kind of resistance. Many times, it comes from the faulty belief that we are unworthy or not enough.

## WHY DO WE RESIST TAKING TIME FOR WHAT WE NEED?

As a child I was oppositional to authority. As I began to awaken and learn and experience myself, I recognized that I was also oppositional to the authority within. I didn't want to listen to my Higher Self. I either ignored her (me) or became oppositional. This was my passive-aggressive defense mechanism to keep myself safe because I was fearful and did not trust anyone, not even myself. This behavior arose from a victim story that I allowed the ego to create.

This unconscious behavior gave me a false reassurance that I had some control over my life. That behavior has decreased over time, but it is still something I continue to work on. Letting go of defense mechanisms is all a part of learning how to accept our perfection in every moment and trust God's goodness, Divine Truth, and guidance.

We simply need to see our resistance as another area that we need to retrain and discipline. Only then can we accept that it is perfectly okay to give ourselves attention, care and follow through with our heart's desires. There are healing messages within the resistance that we need to become aware of. We also need to recognize that there is a loving force within trying to guide us to what is best for us…self-love, compassion, and grace.

*I want to be clear that resistance is not always a hindrance. There are times where resistance is important such as resisting temptations that are not in our best interest. Our intuition needs to guide us in all perceptions and decisions.*

Many of us, especially parents, would not hesitate to take care of another human being or animal if we thought that care and attention were needed. We simply must acknowledge and accept that it is just as important to extend the same kind of loving, caring attention to our Spiritual, physical, and emotional needs as well.

As children, many of us did not get our needs emotionally, Spiritually, or physically met and as a result we neglect our own needs now. As adults we then look to others and to material things to give us a sense of importance and to take care of our emotional, physical, and Spiritual needs. This is a classic example of unconscious, self-rejecting behavior. **You matter!**

We find it is easier to be impulsive and fill our self up with all kinds of distractions, people, and destructive behaviors than it is to take the best possible care of our self. We begin to reverse these familial energetic patterns by working on our deep breathing, centering, listening, and following through with our intuitive guidance without the delay.

If you only knew the Love that lives within you and that you are, you would think that you would not hesitate to follow your guidance. Even when you understand this

## WHY DO WE RESIST TAKING TIME FOR WHAT WE NEED?

Love, following your guidance will always require your faith and trust, because delay and resistance are always present. This is because our false self does not like to give up its 'false sense of control.' It is unable to understand the logic and rationality of what we are being guided to do. The ego thought process always creates some degree of doubt.

> *Stop living from energetic memories*
> *and live from Truth.*
> *- Jesus -*

This quote from Jesus reminds us that we need to stop repeating faulty patterns of thinking, beliefs and behaviors based on the stories from our past programing and live within the Divine Truth that comes to us through our intuition. This describes living *'A **Divinely Ordered Life**.'*

Please remember that all the work that I'm encouraging you to do, constitutes a lifelong journey to find and accept your True inner Self. You can't expect to reach this goal quickly. You can't expect to stay in what you imagine your Highest is all of the time. The journey is accepting that you are perfect in every moment because your Divinity never changes. It's a journey, and some days will be much happier, more comfortable and peaceful than others because life is always happening, and you are caught up in it. Our perception of life needs to expand with Divine Truth to stay in our natural state of joy and happiness.

Everything is always in Divine order and perfect no matter what you are feeling or doing. You are always under God's care whether you know it or not. You are never to judge yourself. You need to keep reminding yourself that this is just an illusion and that you are pure perfection and unconditionally Loved.

> *'I AM One with the Light.*
> *I can never do anything wrong.*
> *I AM eternal Love, and I AM always enough.'*

As we travel down our individual paths, we'll begin to see subtle shifts in our Spiritual growth, the never-ending expansion of our Consciousness. In my clinical practice (and even as I work on myself) we often fail to recognize the amazing progress we are making. Even when we have been able to achieve significant and important progress, we feel that it is still not good enough.

That, my love, is an ego thought from SPEC and it is pervasive through all your thinking. Believe me, even if you may not be able to see your own progress, others do. You need to rely on God to validate you as you keep building your confidence. It is important to remember that it is God transforming you. He oversees what you

## WHY DO WE RESIST TAKING TIME FOR WHAT WE NEED?

call progress. Progress or transformation is not measured by earthly standards. It is Divinely managed. It is important to take the pressure off yourself and let God transform you as He sees fit rather than listening to the ego which is always telling you what it thinks you should be, look like or do. Listening to the ego is the root cause of an identity crisis.

*You want to be in alignment with*
*God's conception of you*
*and what you were created for.*

If you have been reading any of my books, you should be able to recognize the themes or patterns of resistance, delay, stalling, and rebellion that everyone struggles to overcome. If you can't see your own progress, don't panic. That is just your ego judging you. It's all a completely normal part of the process. You must remember that God is moving and working in you every single moment whether you notice it or not. You are already a success, worthy, and everything you hope to be…you just forgot. You are Divine Consciousness.

It has become commonplace in our society to indulge the ego, but we are not taught how to indulge our Soul or Divine intuition. We can begin to see how a sustained belief in separation and detachment from God is so very destructive and disruptive. It creates feelings of rejection and fear. So many of us feel alone, rejected, and abandoned. The more we do the Spiritual work, the more we can accept and believe God's Truth and remember that we are never separated, we are One and the same. God is You!

We are the Divine Self, One Holy Self. Ego only believes in itself. The illusion feels so real because it creates a facade that leads us to feel and believe that we are split in two, a split mind, God mind and Human mind, good and evil, always in conflict with each other. For incarnation purposes, Divine Consciousness takes on the illusion of physical form that we know as the body. This creates our sense of separation and duality. This is why we believe the Divine lives outside of us rather than within.

You can become entangled in a war for control if you try to reason or argue with the ego. As mentioned previously, the more you can just bare witness to the ego and dismiss it rather than getting into a power struggle, the easier your life will become. Engaging with the ego does nothing but trigger frustration, anxiety, and anger. This creates cognitive dissonance. Eventually, you will begin to understand that you are One being and that the ego is simply an illusion of thought.

As you become more centered you will witness these internal dynamics playing out as undercurrents of disobedience and rebelliousness against what is best for your self. The conflict of the two voices has always existed. We know it well as the Angel and the Devil within. You've just never been awake to it. You always thought the ego voice

## WHY DO WE RESIST TAKING TIME FOR WHAT WE NEED?

was your voice and your belief system. You just never had a front row seat before to witness how subtle, complicated, and destructive it can be. You simply need to learn how to listen to, believe in and submit to your intuition rather than the ego.

There is a difference between submitting and being submissive. Many of us are overly submissive to others. This can be tremendously unhealthy and destructive when it comes from a place of wanting to avoid conflict, or from a place of dependency where we don't want to take responsibility for our emotional and sometimes physical self.

Submitting to your intuition (God) is not about dependency or avoidance. It is about doing what is best for you from the perspective of Divine Truth and not from a place of fear. It is a higher level of Consciousness to understand that you share and are One with God's Will.

The more you get into alignment with that Truth the less internal struggle you experience. This is not going to happen overnight, and it doesn't mean that the ego will not continue to exert its influence over you. In submitting to your intuition, you are not giving up control you are gaining everything including control over your mind.

You must want to accept that you are going to have to confront your rebelliousness, disobedience, and delaying behaviors so you can work on and move past them. These behaviors are just coping mechanisms left over from childhood that gave you some sense of control over your environment. If you notice you are not following through with what your intuition is directing you to do, ask your self what might be causing the delay. Process it with your guidance.

---

### Journal Entry 12/27/16
### with God, Goddess and Jesus

---

Although I perceive these Divine entities in separate physical form, I Know they are One. I am with God and the Goddess. They both hold me, permeating me with Love. We are a Holy Trinity as Mother, Father, and Child. I am at God's table. It feels very good and Loving.

**Me:** I want to understand the ego, sacrifice, and suffering. I want to be the biggest vessel of Love, Light and Joy that I can be.

**God:** You already are all these things, Debbie. You just need to keep coming Home to yourself, your Highest. Remember and believe in your Divinity. You still think

## WHY DO WE RESIST TAKING TIME FOR WHAT WE NEED?

you are not enough. It is your ego that believes you are not these things. Sacrifice and suffering are a perspective. You are going to keep rising higher and higher in Consciousness.

**Me:** This is an important reminder that I am not separated from my Self or you, God. It is the illusion of the ego that keeps making me feel I am not plugged-in, because my ego will never feel connected. Thank you for reminding me that whatever I am thinking I am creating. I keep thinking I am not enough in so many areas of my life and therefore deficient in some way. I need to stop compartmentalizing myself and see myself as whole. There is no truth to what my ego is saying. The truth is that I Am enough. I Am everything. I Am Divine Consciousness.

**Jesus:** *We don't have to feel that we are always sacrificing or suffering in some way.* It is the ego that says, "Oh, if only I weren't here, then I could be there." This kind of thinking comes from the ego not wanting to stay present. Yes, there are many things you might like to be doing than what you are doing now. You should only do things you want to do. It is your ego that says you have to do this or have to do that...and that creates suffering.

**Me:** On this earth there are things you must do, like work to earn money.

**Jesus:** Yes, but that is an illusion too. Work does not have to be hard. We don't have to perceive it as being hard or inconvenient. Work can be easy if you are doing something you love, and you can learn to love everything you do, even cleaning, Debbie!

**Me:** So, I just need to be in a state of Love and stay present?

**Jesus:** Yes. It is your ego that perceives things as a drag or misery or an obligation.

**Me:** I am no longer engaged in my clinical practice because I have chosen to write books. Sometimes it feels like I am not helping people.

**Jesus:** You are not cutting yourself off from people to write books. You are working with people all the time. People are reading your books and your posts on-line, and you're helping whomever you come in contact with. All you need to do is shift your perspective. You are also touching everyone in your prayers by sending Light into the world.

*The grace given by God is unconditional, infinite, and eternal. I am in awe of the grace I am given.*

# Chapter Eleven

PROCRASTINATION AND COMMITMENT

*When the smoke settles,
where will you find yourself?*

Many of us have had wonderful dreams or passionate ideas of what we would love to do but have not yet started on them. Perhaps over time we have even forgotten what they were.

While I was writing this book in 2016, I was in the process of relocating our home to another state. I was also in the midst of starting a counseling practice in our new location. I remembered that I had stopped writing for about eight weeks to focus on other things, and for about a week or so I had been hearing from Jesus that it was time to continue writing this book.

At that time, I was trying to rationalize why I didn't need to start writing again. I was still in the process of getting my first three volumes edited, organized, and published. It didn't make sense that I was being asked to continue writing when I already had so many other tasks on my plate. My intuition was energetically pulling me to continue working on this book. Even though I didn't understand the reason, I said 'okay' and got back to my writing.

I noticed that I had been stalling because I didn't understand the reason why I was being directed to resume my writing at that moment. What I ultimately decided was that it doesn't matter, it was okay not to understand. I am not going to understand the big picture of what God has in mind. If I am being led to resume writing, then I know I need to follow through without any questions. My intuition was prompting me to trust my inner voice, recommit to my Spiritual process and follow through.

Even though I had other plans for the day, I understood that God wanted me to resume my writing and nothing else mattered. So, there I sat, writing, recommitting to the Spiritual process, and getting a clearer understanding of how easy it is for me to stray away from listening to my inner guidance.

It is the ego that believes I have more important things to do and is constantly trying to usurp God's Will for its own purpose. When we stay in the present moment, we can learn great lessons from these kinds of situations.

## PROCRASTINATION AND COMMITMENT

As I look back on it now, this incident allowed me to see the taskmaster I had been with myself all my life. I kept taking on more responsibilities than I could handle. I could also see my faulty belief that Divine authority was victimizing me by 'making me do too much.' This faulty thought reinforced the belief that I am not enough. This thought also allowed me to feel like a failure because I was not finishing things in a timely manner. I just had to laugh. God never overwhelms you. He always gives you all the support you need.

*Most of us act out relationship patterns of persecutor, victim, and rescuer all the time, even within our experience of God.*

*You are choosing your experiences and you are also choosing your reaction to them. Many of these experiences are patterns of victim consciousness. You set yourself up for believing you are a failure.*

We really need to be lighthearted about everything we are learning about ourselves. When we don't take our self too seriously, we can see the absurdity of the false self's behaviors and beliefs. Sometimes it is just best to laugh about the hypocrisy of it all. As I have said before, this is a life's journey. What will keep you forging ahead is your dedicated commitment to working on your awakened path because this will ultimately lead you to your Divine purpose with a sense of humor, contentment, and peace.

Whenever you find that stalling or procrastination are taking you off course you must summon up all your persistence and tenacity to recommit yourself to your awakened journey.

Remember, these are built in energies and old behavioral patterns to keep you off course, so it is normal to experience them. Eventually you will recognize that you must step up regularly to balance these energies with Truth and not let them control you. Otherwise, you get sucked back into the trance for longer lengths of time.

As I was writing this book my husband and I had an interesting experience. We lived on a canal and suddenly at high tide our cross-canal neighbor's unmanned 32-foot boat started drifting backward off its lift. The boat was being taken down the canal by wind and currents.

It was about to collide with another docked boat when one of our neighbors saw the impending disaster and was able to jump aboard the wayward vessel. Luckily, the keys were still in the ignition, and she was able to quickly gain control of the boat. She drove the boat back up the canal out of harm's way and returned it safely to its owner. The owner promptly made the necessary adjustments to the height of his boatlift, and what could have been a nasty incident ended harmlessly.

## PROCRASTINATION AND COMMITMENT

I saw this as a metaphor of how we drift away from God, our center. The ego is constantly trying to lure us back into the spell of the trance. God is always beckoning us back Home and helping us navigate back to center.

God is the balancer of all energy. I ask for His help when I realize that my mind has drifted away from being present and He always guides me back and restores my peace. I thought about the lucky coincidence of the keys being left in the ignition. I thought that this was an interesting metaphor about life as well.

The keys to everything are already within us. Yet because we are unconscious, we look outside of ourselves for answers. The interesting thing is that 'our boat' is always being manned from within. We just need to be the awakened co-captain (together with God) of our boat.

We are never really off the boatlift. We are never really floating adrift down the canal. The illusion has us believe we are voyaging alone and subject to all kinds of disappointments and disasters. When we don't understand how secure and protected we are, we go though life crashing into and up against all kinds of things. We can feel victimized by our experiences. We drift backwards into victim consciousness or stay stuck where we are because we don't quiet ourselves enough to hear our intuition. Or, if we do hear it, we ignore it, which always delays our peace.

We are never without a compass. When we learn to get into alignment (believing that we are always guided) with that compass (God) our life is more amazing than you could ever imagine.

Many lack the commitment to staying steady and on course because we rely on our human eyes to see, our human mind to understand, and the ego's irrational beliefs to direct us. The Truth is, that until we can access our inner guidance, our intuition, we need to rely on trust and faith that Divine presence is always within trying to get our attention and correcting our perceptions.

We do not know what is best for us or what our unique journey is about. Only the Divine does. We need to give up thinking that we know everything because the concepts and programming learned on Earth have no truth to them. It takes time to embrace this understanding.

I still question God at times when He asks me to do something. Like a little child being defiant with its parent, I want to know 'why?' I am still working on this, but I can assure you He never gets upset or angry when I am defiant or rebellious. He thinks it is cute! He smiles at me and laughs! The Grace that we are given is beyond anything I can describe.

You must rely on trust and faith in God's goodness because you cannot see the whole picture; it is too expansive for your mind. There are forces within, greater than you can imagine that Love you and know what is best for you. Your story and path are already written and complet-

## PROCRASTINATION AND COMMITMENT

ed. Believing this Truth helps you to stay committed to your Spiritual path.

Blind faith is difficult to accept, but it is also necessary if you are to accomplish your purpose in life in a peaceful manner. Even Jesus said that those who can stay in faith without being able to see miracles are truly blessed. In time, you will develop an intimate relationship with your Creator and your faith won't be 'blind' anymore. You Know you are Loved unconditionally, and that God is good and has your best interest at heart. You are His/your Conscious Creation.

He has a magnificent role for you to play and wants to ready you for it. In the meantime, it can be a challenge to commit to this road due to all the illusionary energies escorting you. Mastering your internal world (mind) is not for everyone. Awakening is not for sissies.

If you are reading this book, then something within you Knows that this is a commitment you must make. If you have taken the necessary steps to open to your Divine guidance, then you have a constant companion helping you to stay committed and to recommit to this process when necessary. Your guides are always cheering you on and want you to unfold into your Divine destiny happily and peacefully on Earth...remembering who you are!

I am constantly being 'nudged' until I take steps to do what I am being asked or directed to do. I will tell you that, as uncomfortable as it might be, those 'nudges' won't go away until you follow through. Every time I follow through, I am thrilled with what I was asked to do and wonder why it took me so long.

At times you'll look at the nudge as being relentless and a bother and you'll want to rebel, like when God would constantly wake me up at night for a Divine teaching and I told Him to stop waking me up! I liked my sleep! I was a handful, but it never changed His patience and His unconditional Love for me.

When you're feeling this kind of rebelliousness, you must recognize that this is only your ego…or a younger version of yourself having one of its temper tantrums. You can rebel if you want, but a better choice is to follow through, feel blessed and Loved Knowing that you are not alone on your journey. God is moving through you.

## Journal Entry 2/22/15
### With my Higher Self

This journal entry describes what it is like to do Inner Child work. At the time, I was just starting to understand how I self-abandoned and separated from myself by rejecting younger parts of me. This was due to my experiencing emotional and physical abuse as a child and sexual abuse as a teenager. We all have unhealed parts of us that still exert control over us today. Most of us are unaware of this, especially if we have had trauma in our life. All these aspects of our self need to be healed and integrated with acceptance, compassion, and Love. I can't imagine doing this work without the help of Divine guidance.

**Me:** This is what I figured out. My will to control is tremendously strong. Thank you, God, for showing me this in my dreams. I understand that you tried to show me this with my client the other day. Having to accept and deal with the issues surrounding my Florida license, my ego took over. I wanted to control the outcome. I was singing "I don't have to take a test" like a spoiled child, not ever thinking I would have to take more college credits! Silly me! I was so frustrated, angry, irritated, and disappointed with the situation and what I witnessed and *misperceived* was a very ugly part of me. When I am feeling this way or even startled, I react to fear with anger in order to control, to stay safe. I understand that this is a huge block and I noticed it before in different ways, but now it stands out. I understand that to move forward and grow more, I need to give up my ego will and depend on you to lead me and handle my problems. I do not want to react in a manner that I am not proud of and do not want to be part of my character. It is ugly. Higher Self, how did you break this ugly habit?

**Higher Self**: This is not easy. It's what we learned growing up. We were always on guard because we did not feel safe. But we are safe now. No one is trying to hurt us. Furthermore, we do not want to judge these behaviors. There is nothing wrong with them. You are innocent and you are judging how fear affects you.

**Me**: How do I get rid of that guardedness or fear?

**Higher Self**: We must work more with the little ones, our younger selves (inner child) keeping them feeling safe and loved.

**Me**: How do I do this? I have tried to bring them into my meditation daily to love them as much as I can.

**Higher Self**: We need to do it more often. Let's try it before bed.

**Me**: Is there a specific age me that I am missing or not identifying that needs my attention?

**Higher Self**: Yes, we just had flashes of them in your mind. By age eight, we endured so much battering we were emotionally exhausted. We were so unhappy because of the way that dad and mom treated us that we were held back that year. We even wet our self in class because we were too scared to ask to go to the bathroom. Mom and dad divorced at age eleven. You were very frightened, scared, and angry. Your whole life changed.

**Me:** I have forgotten about all of that. So, I need to focus on these ages of me too? I looked through old pictures of myself from childhood. From age five and up I seem very sad. By age twelve I was very angry and standoffish to dad.

**Higher Self:** Yes, all parts of us need attention. You need to be loving to them throughout the day by being aware of how you are feeling. These younger parts of you are controlling you because they needed then, and still need now, to be acknowledged, healed, and accepted as perfect and integrated. Although our life is just a story, these younger versions of our self believe they experienced situations and feel them to be real.

**Me:** I also noticed that when I was crying earlier it was a very young part of me that thought she was bad for feeling angry (age nine). There is so much complexity and diversity within me. These are all just energetic memories.

# INTUITION

### Journal Entry 9/7/16
### with Jesus

**Me:** It was difficult to let go of my feelings yesterday. I see how strongly I was affected from childhood through age twenty because I was feeling unwanted and thought it was my job to make others happy. My inner rebellion is extremely prominent. I keep pushing my Spirit down making other peoples' needs more important than mine. I just need to keep listening to my intuition because otherwise I am victimizing myself and it takes my strength and Knowingness away. Jesus, I don't want to rebel against myself anymore. I just need to allow myself to be happy; nothing is wrong.

**Jesus:** We love you, Debbie.

**Me:** How do I stop this rebellion in me?

**Jesus:** Ah, this is a good question. This is not easy. Your inner rebellion is a terrific power struggle that arose from how adults used their power in dealing with you, and how the strong will of your ego rebelled against it.

## PROCRASTINATION AND COMMITMENT

It is not just you, my love. All humans have this struggle within, some more than others. It takes time. Continue to Know the voice of your Highest, your intuition, and start obeying it because it is your voice. Look at it this way, every time you disobey it's that little angry fearful child in you that doesn't want to hear anything.

**Me:** Yes, I can look at it that way.

**Jesus:** It is like having children that refuse to listen to you when you know what is best for them. Remember, you are never being judged; you are Loved completely. This is a matter of learning to trust God and be loving and patient with yourself.

**Me:** Okay. So, what would be most loving to myself right now?

**Jesus:** You just had an image flash in front of you. What did you see?

**Me:** I saw myself taking a light-treatment for my skin condition and using a Netipot for my sinuses.

**Jesus:** Great. Let's do it!

## Chapter Twelve

YOUR RESPONSIBILITY TO YOU

*Many times, we seek out hope and healing, but we come up empty because we have not learned how to listen or receive.*

What a joy to Know that we don't have to look any further than within our self. This reminds us that it is our job to learn how to trust our self and not rely on the judgments of other people. It reminds us that God is the fulfiller of all our needs.

Remember, we each have our own Divine curriculum created for our individual experience. It is like a Divine Individual Educational plan. Therefore, each of us has our own path, lessons, Wisdom and purpose in this life and it is only God who can teach it to us. It is joy to Know that we are the only adult for whom we are emotionally responsible. Our Oneness with God gives us the gift of Love. We can then share it with everyone else. When we share our Love with others, it expands and extends our joy.

If you have been taking responsibility for everyone else and not yourself you need to stop, reassess what you are doing, and discuss with them that you are making changes to take care of you. This may create conflict, but it is important to stand your ground. If you feel guilty, you must recognize that is simply the ego beating you up again and it will continue if you allow the programing and conditioning of faulty beliefs to govern your life.

I'm not saying that you can disregard all your adult responsibilities. Perhaps you are caring for an elderly parent. You still need to accept these important responsibilities. But you need to set boundaries and ask others for help, especially God, so He can lead you to care-take with joy. Otherwise, you run the risk of getting caught up once again in your own personal pattern of feeling anxious, angry, burnt out, stuck, trapped, obligated, suffering, martyrdom, and victimization. There is always support, you are never trapped.

If you are taking care of your self and listening to your intuition, it will show you how to go about any task in ways you can perform with joy, ease, and Love. Your instincts will tell you when and where to get extra help and where to set boundaries. You only need to listen to your intuition and then follow through. Ask God for help and you will be surrounded by Earth Angels. You have your own personal Divine GPS system that Knows what is best for you.

Recognize in advance that your ego will try to turn you away from listening to and following your inner knowledge. You can rest assured that your ego will try to bully or deceive you by insisting that tasks must be done a certain way. Don't listen! Ego is just there to give you contrast which at times creates conflict within. It helps you discern the difference between separation and Oneness. Typically, the ego's suggestions do not create a sense of peace; only God provides that.

Other people may make helpful suggestions as to how you should approach a given situation. Don't reject them outright, but always remember to use discernment when listening to other people's suggestions. Bring them to your Divine guidance and then decide what is best.

I don't want you to think that other people are not necessary in your life. Remember that God is working through everyone and everything. There are messages everywhere for us. We are all here to share our Love and Light and enjoy our life, family, friends, community, and the gifts of this magical world. Our intuition Knows best what will make us happiest. When we trust and follow our intuition things will work out best for everyone around us even though it does not always appear to be that way.

## INTUITION

Even when we are following Divine guidance, the Ego will chime in with stories about how it will not be good for others or that we will be rejected. But again, this is from ego and there is no truth to it. There are no mistakes everything is accounted for and in Divine control. What is best for you will ultimately be the best for others.

Throughout your lifetime the ego has used the recycled SPEC to concoct a spider's web of complicated storylines in your mind. So many thoughts and feelings become joined together in an incredibly complicated mental mosaic. It is easy for ego to entangle us in a web of irrational and illusionary conflict and keep us in a delusional trance.

You feel like you are divided into two parts, one ego the other Divine and these parts appear to always be in conflict with each other. However, there is no division within you, no separation. You are only One, there is truly only One Voice, and you are Divine. It just takes time to believe and integrate Truth.

Our storylines and faulty beliefs are so complicated that it becomes difficult to follow each one back to its original source. Navigating through all the storylines becomes problematic. It is better to let go of the story of why, how, when etc. and use your deep breathing techniques to get your self back to center…otherwise you get caught in an endless spiral of drifting back in time. Unless you are working on a specific healing or past trauma, **STAY OUT OF THE PAST!** Once that is done, you can then refocus to seek the Truth from your intuition, your Divine Self.

It is easier to receive direction from our intuition when we come from a place of peace and open heart. The only thing we really need to do is to learn how to be happy and be at peace with our self and our journey. We do this when we believe God's Truth over everything else. When nothing is making sense or we are unsure of everything, we must have the composure to go to our quiet place inside and ask how to proceed and let go.

This doesn't have to be as hard as we make it. We are constantly getting distracted from our center, our quiet place of Knowing, and at times it can take a lot of focused effort to bring ourselves back. It is okay. Just keep refocusing on the present and the Knowledge that there is a healing Love within that wants to envelope us in Light. Allow it.

Remember your life is in Divine order and you are perfect in every moment regardless of how you are feeling, acting, or judging yourself. Deep breathing techniques will always refocus you and bring you back to present and feeling more centered.

The state of confusion or upset you are feeling is just an alert system reminding you that you left Home and need to return. Your feelings are informing you all the time. So, when you realize that you've lost your center and

## INTUITION

got sucked back into the abyss again, simply stop, relax, and take some deep breaths. You will quickly be on your way back Home to your inner peace and intuition.

We can count on life distracting us away from our center each and every day, actually moment by moment. That will never stop. As I mentioned before, the trance is an energetic pull much like gravity, but it is pulling us away from the very things we need and love to do. The ego spins its tales of woe, so we get stuck in our head thinking about all of life's worries. We then get caught in the trance, listening to made-up stories including an irrational rulebook based on faulty programing.

The trick is to master the art of pulling your self back out of the abyss, back to center. Remaining present is a skill that you must practice each day. Don't be hard on your self as you discover how often you slip back into the trance/unconsciousness or fall back into believing the ego's storyline. It is what it is. This will happen the rest of your life, yet the ego's affect on you will become less and less.

> *Your task is to master the awareness that you have strayed away from being present, and then bring yourself back. Because when you are present, you can discern the Truth about what you are experiencing through your physical senses, thoughts, feelings, or beliefs.*

## YOUR RESPONSIBILITY TO YOU

This ability to catch yourself when you drift, in and of itself, should bring you joy and comfort. Overtime, you will be able to stay present for much longer periods of time, although, the trance is always energetically looming.

Think about this for a moment. If we spend time monitoring how well we are staying connected to the present, how can we possibly have time to worry about things or others we are not responsible for?

We can't monitor or bring others back to their center. We have no clue about what is going on with them internally. It is each person's responsibility to do that for themselves. We just need to offer compassion. Become a bridge of Love by holding a space of Love versus judging. See them as the same Divine presence as you are Knowing that God is working within them as well.

What is even more exciting is when we work on this process of developing an intimate relationship with God, we understand that God is always Divinely expanding our perceptions and helping us return Home when we drift. When we believe Divine Truth, we no longer need to micromanage others or our self. This leaves us free to Love ourselves and others wholly and allow everyone to be their authentic Self…Divine perfection.

INTUITION

Journal Entry 6/21/15
Meditation with Jesus

When writing the journal entry below, I was in the midst of taking an awesome graduate class called Multicultural Counseling. The class was taught by Dr. Jason Gines at The Pennsylvania State University. I needed this class to transfer my mental health license from Pennsylvania to Florida. This class shook me to the core and made me re-evaluate all my programmed beliefs about diversity and suffering in the world. The next two journal entries contain profoundly sensitive material because I am being blatantly honest about my experience. Many of my beliefs at the time were coming from a place of Spiritual unconsciousness.

These journal entries are from an earlier stage of my Spiritual journey, before I understood that everything reflects what is within me. I didn't understand that everything we experience has a purpose and is in Divine order, whether it makes sense at the time, or not. At that early stage in my journey, I didn't trust my own feelings and needed someone else to verify them. This was a huge growth experience for me, realizing that what I was feeling was okay and that I can rely on my intuition.

We victimize, persecute, and rescue our own self as we act out our 'story' on the stage of what we call life. If our life seems as though it were a battle, it's because it is simply a mirror image of the battle that is constantly going on between our Highest Self and the ego. It is the dissonance from the perceived duality within. All that conflict is being reflected back to us in the chaos that we perceive in our external world that we find difficult to understand. The core of the conflict comes from our faulty belief in the illusion of life and the separation of all things. We fail to understand that we are never separate from anything.

Our world will change, as we individually accept the unity that needs to co-exist among all the diverse aspects within ourselves and allow our Highest, to oversee this diversity. This conflict results from not understanding that we are Divinely perfect as we are, even with all the diversity that appears to exist within us, between us, and among us. When the belief of separation is healed, we will awaken to the beautiful Truth of our unity, our Oneness with our Creator and everything in the Universe.

**Me:** The world is a complex place. There is so much good and there is so much suffering. In my Multicultural Counseling class, when I read books and articles on the topic of 'white privilege' I had the sense that it was propaganda, using the educational system to sway young, impressionable students to advance the political agenda of the radical left, or

Socialism. I believed the texts and articles were written to inform people about the sufferings of others in a way that is designed to make the reader feel anger and guilt and instill aggression for political and social change by singling out an identifiable class of people who are to blame. I did not believe in the way the authors describe social justice and how the social problems should be fixed.

I believe that much of what is said about the oppression of "target groups" is true, and that many truly experience suffering and oppression. I even understand why minority groups feel that there is such a thing as "white privilege." I did not feel guilt even though I believe the writers would like 'white' readers to feel this way. I felt compassion, but not guilt. However, my interpretation of the readings made me angry and defensive because I felt like I was being singled out, victimized, blamed, and persecuted because I am white. Jesus, am I wrong in the way that I feel?

**Jesus:** How can you be wrong about the way you feel? I do not know what you mean.

**Me:** I guess I am not communicating well. I am asking you if I am missing the point of what I am reading and whether I am close-minded to a different perspective that might be a legitimate way to change things regarding oppression.

## YOUR RESPONSIBILITY TO YOU

**Jesus:** Debbie, you are not being close-minded. You are simply getting defensive in reaction to your feeling that you are personally being blamed.

**Me:** Am I missing the point?

**Jesus:** No, you are understanding the suffering of the world.

**Me:** Am I being close hearted about the situation?

**Jesus:** What do you think?

**Me:** I guess when I take things personally, I am not open to listening or receiving. I believe I can be compassionate about societal rules, but it appears the authors of these papers are looking to achieve a kind of social utopia through ways I am not convinced are right. I feel we should all learn to love and accept one another and our differences, and I pray for world peace and the end to violence. Does being Spirituality awakened mean that you give up things that you believe are not wrong? I do not want to give up my lifestyle, I feel I worked hard, and God gave me blessings to have what He has given me for a reason. What I am understand from the readings in the class is that all white people have accumulated things unjustly because of "white privilege" and slavery. We are not entitled to what we have because it was taken unfairly, and we need to share with others, so everyone has exactly the same power, the same wealth, the same property. On an individual level, I don't even understand how I might be taking power from someone who is not white. I don't mind sharing and I believe my taxes are doing some of that, but certainly not to the extent that these authors want. Is it that I fear losing the material things that I accumulated? Or is it that I am not trusting that God will bring me my dreams?

**Jesus:** Do not let this shake your confidence, Deb. Life is not fair in many ways. When God created man and woman they were expected to live in God's Will and not their own. That is not what happened. Your will is still based in fear like everyone else's. You, Debbie, turn to God to help understand His Will to move forward, but not everyone does this. This is what it takes. Everyone needs to turn to God to understand themselves, their situation, and others.

**Me:** So, everyone is acting from his or her ego?

**Jesus:** Yes, most people.

**Me:** But some people live in horrible places and are oppressed.

**Jesus:** Many cultures do not want change.

**Me:** Some people do and can't get out or away from their circumstances.

**Jesus:** Yes, that is true, but they are suffering for a reason.

**Me:** What is that reason?

**Jesus:** So, others can learn.

**Me:** Learn what?

**Jesus:** To not be passive with themselves.

**Me:** I need to work on not letting my emotions control me when I discuss something I feel passionate about. I am very conscious of my ability to raise my cortisol level and I see it and feel it when I speak in that class. I need to come from a place of peace. I can sometimes get overexcited and say things in anger that I shouldn't. How does one view all these situations if we are not of this world?

**Jesus:** There is suffering everywhere, internally, and externally. It is because of the ego. We oppress ourselves and others. We are individually responsible for our actions toward our self and others.

**Me:** What are we supposed to learn from watching suffering in a third-world country, where people have no way out?

**Jesus:** It is the same thing as in your mind.

**Me:** What do you mean?

**Jesus:** When people see, or feel, or experience suffering and oppression, the only thing they can do is pray for God's help to end their suffering. People become violent when they feel pushed to the edge. They take things into their own hands and then they oppress or kill others. All the suffering is created in our minds.

**Me:** Some countries are very religious and pray.

**Jesus:** Yes, but it is not the right time, you will not understand yet. There is a great deal of violence today, although there has always been violence. People don't want violence, but they still want to control everything. They do not look to God to heal them.

**Me:** So, watching others suffer and witnessing violence is to help us see that we should not do this anymore to ourselves or others?

# YOUR RESPONSIBILITY TO YOU

**Jesus:** Yes. Do you remember when you learned that we see things not as they are, but as an illusion, a projection from the ego, a mirror image that gets played out on the outside?

**Me:** Yes. I believed that I was suffering for a very long time from childhood experiences. There was a pattern of suffering and violence in my home. I see, so my pain is being played out on the Earth stage.

**Jesus:** Well, the same goes for looking at groups, countries, and the world. We need to pray that God heals each of us individually and all of us collectively.

**Me:** What is my role in understanding or doing?

**Jesus:** It is to pray for peoples' suffering to end. You need to be happy, loving, and compassionate. Be open to other people's ideas, at least they are trying to fix the situation even if it may not be in the correct way. They see a problem and want to help fix it, but it will only happen with God's help. Each person must search within to understand how best to help the greater good. I love you, Debbie. These are good questions, but there are no easy answers.

**Me:** I recognize that I have been shaped by my family, transmitted energy, relationships, experiences, society, and education. It is my job to let go of all that programming and be reshaped by God. I pushed my feelings of loneliness, isolation, and despair down for many years, and did not acknowledge them. The Multicultural Counseling class triggered so much loneliness, despair, separation, and isolation in me that I felt disconnected and insecure. I guess this class was 'Spiritually purposeful' and meant to bring up feelings and thoughts within me that needed to be healed. My twelve and fifteen-year-old selves became present in me. That part of my life needed to be acknowledged, processed, healed, and released.

**Jesus:** You were justified in feeling that way as a child, but we do not have to feel this way anymore. Minorities need their pain acknowledged so they can move forward. It is God's job to help them move forward with their pain, just like He is doing with your pain right now.

**Me:** How do we process our pain or acknowledge it if our home is not safe, if being alone with our pain is so difficult that we need to distract our self with work, addictions or people? How do children who feel pain and shame, regardless of the reason why, process their pain when they are not feeling safe?

## YOUR RESPONSIBILITY TO YOU

**Jesus:** Things aren't fair. You can look everywhere, and everyone can finger point at some group that feels entitled and takes advantage of others.

**Me:** The government is a good example of that.

**Jesus:** This is life.

**Me:** Why is it this way?

**Jesus:** Greed. **Greed and Spiritual unconsciousness.** Everyone wants what someone else has and will do whatever it takes to get it.

**Me:** How did it get this way?

**Jesus:** Lack of belief in God coupled with fear and a wish for power to make one stronger than others. This is the ego in charge.

**Me:** But some cultures have nothing, not even basic needs.

**Jesus:** Yes, that is true.

**Me:** It appears that white people have so much compared to what some other cultures/races have, and those cultures want it given to them or at least to have the same opportunities.

**Jesus:** Yes, they should have the same opportunities, without fear.

**Me:** Some of these cultures though refuse to educate themselves, or do not understand the importance of work to earn money. What then?

**Jesus:** This is not something you can fix.

**Me:** How do you give people work that don't know the basics.

**Jesus:** You educate them.

**Me:** Yes, but many disregard the education given to them. It does feel hopeless. What am I not seeing?

**Jesus:** You are not seeing the bigger picture. People need hope in order to learn and to commit to their progress. White people have been given a leg up so they can teach these other cultures.

**Me:** How do we do this?

**Jesus:** By sharing information, teaching, and helping all children receive the same education.

**Me:** Minorities are taught the same as white children.

**Jesus:** They are not.

**Me:** I don't understand.

**Jesus:** I know this is a complex and difficult.

**Me:** What is different?

**Jesus:** Many are not given the same support at home for education. Their families never received that support either.

**Me:** This happens with white Appalachia as well.

**Jesus:** Yes, it is the same problem. We assume that these children have been habituated the same way middle class America has, but that just isn't true. Their cultural influences have been very different and therefore, they are starting at a different point of learning. Some children can never even be certain about their safety or whether they will have a basic meal in a day, or a bed to sleep in at night. They begin life with different experiences…one where the most basic needs are not being met.

**Me:** So how can a child learn when their basic needs are not taken care of? How do you make it fun and safe for children to learn? I never thought of things this way, but it makes total sense. I can look at how my experiences shaped my inability to pay attention in school. It was not good. I lived in fear and anxiety about what was happening at home and what will happen next. I didn't feel safe, and it kept me distracted from listening and focusing in school even though my basic needs were being met. I know that we cannot change the school system.

**Jesus:** Yes, that is not going to fly.

**Me:** We don't want the education curriculum made too easy either that would not make sense.

**Jesus:** No, it does not.

**Me:** We can't go into people's homes and make sure their basic needs are met, can we?

**Jesus:** Not really, even though that is what the system is trying to do.

**Me:** Then what is the suggestion to improve the chances of children being able to rise with education?

## YOUR RESPONSIBILITY TO YOU

**Jesus:** It isn't easy. Can you think of anything?

**Me:** I guess the point is how to make children feel safe in a learning environment to stay focused and achieve no matter what they have going on at home.

**Jesus:** Yes, that would be a good start.

**Me:** Maybe teaching children focusing skills, mindfulness, emotional regulation, connection to their Higher being, relaxation skills to feel peaceful while they learn. Teaching them to take responsibility for their own feelings and behaviors by learning how to process them.

**Jesus:** That sounds wonderful!

**Me:** How can this happen?

**Jesus:** Teaching. Teaching these skills to teachers, schools, and students. Teaching a curriculum of relaxation to promote a more positive learning environment.

**Me:** Are you saying that I would do this?

**Jesus:** Yes, we will work on this as you keep developing. It will empower all individuals to assume responsibility for their own emotions, growth and worth. This way they can rise above the conditions at home like you did. You will have lots of help with this, Debbie. You do not need to worry. You and I will work on the details.

Journal entry 8/9/16

I woke up this morning and realized that since all time is happening simultaneously then I have already achieved my goals of what I want to do or who I want to be. I do not have to worry or force it. My life is unfolding daily. I need to enjoy the process and just allow it to unfold. Being patient with the process is a journey in itself and has to do with trusting and having faith in God. I can accept that I Am everything I ever wanted to be and more in this moment. Everything happens when it is supposed to...in Divine time.

## YOUR RESPONSIBILITY TO YOU

Journal Entry 6/26/2020
A Message from God about Preferences

Does someone have to be wrong for you to be right? Do you automatically feel as if you are wrong when someone else believes they are right?

We can take a giant step towards Oneness if we allow each person to have an individual preference. Practicing this concept is a great opportunity to open and expand your mind. Understand that each person is in a different place in their journey to attain Higher Consciousness. To live in a world with peace and harmony we need to live in an *internal* world of allowing differences. You are a complex being. It is difficult to negotiate the myriad of thoughts, beliefs, and feelings within.

We are learning not to resist the complexity and contrast of thoughts, beliefs, and feelings within. We still need to look at them to understand the origin of each and to see if they are rational.

## INTUITION

Each moment you get an opportunity to check in with Me to help you sort through the complexity and contrast with Higher Truth. Are you willing to do that rather than relying on your own judgment of how to perceive and proceed and where to put your energy?

You must accept yourself first before you can accept others. Until you can do this there will be a judgmental war going on within you which, as you know, will be reflected in your outer world. There is innocence and goodness in everyone, but you must see it in your own self first.

You are all beautiful...Creation's creation. I have created everyone equally and each of you has a part to play in helping others to go higher in their awakening...to return to the Oneness of Love. Your sisters and brothers are helping you see the things you don't like about yourself that you are constantly projecting onto others.

The peace is within. It is yours; it is a given. It is My eternal gift to you. Rest in Me. Let me help you navigate your trials and together we will bring more Love and Light into this world. See through the lens of Love Knowing everything is in Divine Providence for the highest good of all, even if it looks otherwise. I am always shifting your awareness to expand your Consciousness.

## YOUR RESPONSIBILITY TO YOU

Letting go of faulty belief systems is an ongoing process. Become open and allow yourself to observe without judgment. It is the key in your growth. Examine the rational of each belief and ask yourself, is this my truth? Most of the time you will find it is not.

I Love all of my creation. It is time to fully Love yourself with all your beautiful complexity if you want to Love and accept everyone else. However, I want you to keep in mind that you are always going to have preferences. Going higher means that you remain open to accepting everyone's subjective experience and of how they go about their journey. It takes great grace and acceptance...like a parent watching and allowing their child to make its own decisions to find out who they truly are. Others do not have to be wrong for you to be right and you do not have to wrong for others to be right. Love the journey.

## Chapter Thirteen

BELIEVING IN YOUR SELF

*How extraordinary we could be
if only we listened within and believed
and understood who we are and that
we are already where we long to be.*

Through the awakening process you are learning to Love and believe in your Self. You are realizing that the more you believe in your Self, the more you want to listen and follow through with your intuition because you trust that there is perfect Wisdom within you. You realize that resisting that Wisdom no longer makes sense.

*As you overcome ego pride, you see that you
are only fighting the guiding light of Wisdom
that is within you. It means laying down
the sword of control and letting go. It means*

# INTUITION

*believing and accepting the Divine Truth, power, and guidance within.*

*This Light is you. It is the source of who you are. It is your essence, the Spirit of God, Divine Consciousness. It Knows what is ideal for you and leads you to your purpose. It is the safety net within and without.*

As humans, we constantly seek outside validation. Everyone wants to be seen and feel that they are important. Many of us continue to struggle with feelings of unworthiness and therefore, we don't believe in our Self as we should. We need to listen to our inner Wisdom even though we still feel uncomfortable and unsure. Our journey is also about trusting and believing in our Self, not just trusting, and believing in God; for we are One with our Creator.

*Know the Truth of who you are and let that validate you.*

Your intuition is your best friend; it is you, your Highest Self, the Creator. Getting into a Loving trusting relationship with your Self is very important as your Consciousness continues to expand. You must believe and apply the Wisdom you are learning. You are being polished for your Divine calling. You are crucial in your

Creator's plan for His deliverance of the world, which is the restoration and deliverance of you.

As you start to follow your intuition you will find that you become more authentic because you don't have to put on airs or control every interaction that you have. You can remove your mask. You are happy and content with simply being you. Your 'performance' in a sense is over. You are free to be you because you no longer feel that there is something wrong with you. You accept that you are worthy just by being your amazing self. That means who you are right now, your authentic self, not who you think you should be. You realize that you are perfection right now and in every moment. This is stepping into your power, your Divine authenticity, and it is freedom.

The belief in your Self is not just that you can do things or are capable. It is the realization that you are an inherently good person, that you are innocent, and that you genuinely like who you are. You can see your own Light, Love, Wisdom and Divine beauty as the God within. ***You enjoy being you right now without further transformation.***

As this occurs the pressure to micro-manage everything you do is released. You believe that you are whole and need nothing else to feel that way. You also recognize that everyone else is whole and One with God, regardless of what your senses or ego tells you. You are now plugged into your own Divinity because you have accepted and believe Divine Truth.

INTUITION

*Divinity bows to itself in honor and reverence, for all of Creation recognizes its Oneness.*

The relationship you have with your Self will be the most important relationship you will ever have. This becomes the framework for every relationship you have with the external world. To develop a relationship with your Self, you need to participate in an intimate relationship with God. God teaches you who you are. He helps you Know yourself through your Divine identity. When you are in awakened communion with God you learn that you are perfect just as you are.

*You are a perfect reflection of God's Light because you are a conscious Creation of Love.*

*Everything that you lay your eyes upon is a conscious Creation of Love. Everything is God, Divine Consciousness.*

*- Holy communion -*
*Is your union with Love Itself*

I remember when I first saw a visual image of my Higher Self. I saw her as separate from myself. I was blown away by the Love, Wisdom and care she had for me. I fell in Love with her (me) and wanted to emulate her to learn how to be and feel like her. It has actually taken a long time to integrate and understand that my Higher Self is not a separate being. She is me...Divine essence in form.

The ego has you view your Higher Self as separate. It is not. I can visually see and hear my Higher Self and have learned that I am seeing myself as I am, in physical form, already transformed. I see the image of me, my Divine Self, through God's eyes rather than through the eyes of the ego.

It is very reassuring to Know that I am already there, although it is easy to forget whenever I slip back into the trance. That is when I feel the need to accelerate my transformation because in that moment, I forgot that I Am Divine perfection. I must get back into alignment with Divine Truth. This urgency is created by ego because it does not believe that I am already transformed or perfect as I am. It lives in the fear of missing out or that I will run out of time before my transformation is complete. When I felt this urgency, it started a cycle of 'doing' in an effort to make my vision of my future happen sooner. I was lacking faith and did not truly understand Divine timing or how the incarnation works.

This cycle of doing is fueled by faulty beliefs that create a sense that you have internal or external blockages that are holding you back. This feeling is steeped in the belief that you are not where you are supposed to be and 'not enough'. If you are present, this 'doing cycle' gives you the opportunity to become aware that you are caught up in an ego process that is attempting to control your life. Ego makes you believe that you are stuck or trapped.

The only thing that needs to be healed or cleared is your faulty beliefs, as they become a barrier to your happiness. Your awareness is a great opportunity to let go of these limiting beliefs and accept your perfection. God is in control of your path and timing. You decide how you want to experience it...pressure fueled by fear or with ease.

I learned a method that I used to connect with my Higher Self from one of Dr. Margaret Paul's web-based workshops on increasing your vibration. It helped me to be able to visually see my Higher self. I mentioned this tool earlier, it is called Visual Guided Imagery and it accesses your imagination. During meditation you can ask your Higher Self to show itself to you or to help you hear its guidance. Remember, some people hear, feel or Know Divine guidance, while others see images.

The ability to visualize or hear your Higher Self is the same as hearing your intuition. It is just another form of the same Divine guidance that helps you keep moving on your journey of awakening. With visualization you are giving form to your intuition, to your God self. Many times, the visual images are metaphors about Higher- learning. I highly recommend visual guided imagery as a meditation technique to help you see the Truth of who you are. To read the specific meditation I used please check out the book "*Do I have to Give Up Me to Be Loved by God?* – by Dr. Margaret Paul. You will find the guided meditation on page 177. God has given us so many creative ways to remember to return Home to Love.

*Divine Consciousness is
creative imagination.*

I used this technique with many of my clients. Most saw their Higher Self as beautiful, healthy, and transformed. They saw themselves as the Divine perfection that they already are. Most of them also heard guidance and felt Divine Love. It helped them to learn how to accept, Love and believe in themselves as a Divine being. It is a gift from God to be able to awaken, see, feel and Know the expansive Love that you are.

It was reassuring for them to learn of the Divine support accompanying them on their journey. They found their way Home to their Divine Self, the Light, Love and Oneness of God for a moment. Now that they had the necessary tools, I recommended that they establish a daily practice of guided imagery on their own in addition to what we practiced in therapy sessions.

This life experience is about awakening and remembering who you truly are, Knowing and feeling the wholeness of being One within your Self, as God, as Creation. It is amazing when you finally experience the pure bliss of being Home, wrapped in the Love and Oneness of God.

Integrating Divine Wisdom and staying in a state of expanded Consciousness takes a lot of time and effort as you go about your busy days. It is easy to slip back into unconsciousness. When you catch yourself drifting, smile and give yourself a pat on the back. Don't become frustrated. It is all part of the process and experience. It takes time, patience, and practice, yet you have so much Divine intervention as guidance every day. No pressure. Each day, remember who you are and keep believing in All that you are. More treasures will come from within.

## Journal Entry 7/10/17
### With King Solomon who has been working with me on the art of 'allowing.'

**Me:** I know I need to keep allowing everything I am perceiving in the external world and understand it's just an illusion. Unfortunately, that doesn't help when I feel pain because of what I am seeing. It is confusing walking between the Spiritual world and a world of duality and not always knowing what to do. I guess that is why you keep telling me to allow and feel. All I really need to do is experience and remember Divine Truth. Can you please help me with this King Solomon?

**King Solomon:** This is such a beautiful question, Debbie. This is hard. You are respecting others' wishes and not trying to force your agenda on them. You must keep remembering this is their journey, and it is okay no matter what it looks like. Your love needs to allow all. Let people be who they are. You are at a difficult stage in letting go of more of your ego beliefs and we are here to help you. Keep leaning on us just like you are right now. You don't understand the whole picture.

**Me:** What about terrible things that happen, like events you see on the news?

**King Solomon:** You cannot control it, so you need to let go of it. Allowing does not mean something is right or wrong. It just means letting it be instead of judging it. Instead, you can say, "I don't fully understand what I am seeing or why I am seeing it" and then let go and pray if that helps you.

**ME:** It has come to my mind many times how easy it is to have a lack of grace for myself and others, and I wonder how God does it. I am always walking in a state of grace and Love from God, Jesus, and the Angels. Never once did I ever feel anything different no matter what I think, believe, do, or don't do. There is infinite and eternal patience and forgiveness through God's grace. I try to remind myself to receive this grace as it is given, and then extend it to myself and others. I can do it when I remember, although, I am human, and I forget and make mistakes.

**King Solomon:** Wouldn't we all love to get a second chance, Debbie, a do-over? Well, here it is. The process of awakening over and over again throughout the day is a continuous second chance for you and others to be present and who you were meant to be, a blessing, not who you thought you had to be.

This is cosmic grace. You get a second chance to be the Love and Light you were created to be. Will you grab that chance, or will you not trust it, just like you haven't trusted other things in your life? Will you let go of your illusionary suffering, the delusion, your story, or will you cling to it? Your choices will make a difference in how you experience the rest of your life.

Debbie, how does clinging to the illusion benefit you and others? Don't you prefer freedom for yourself and the rest of the world? Your act of letting go will influence others to seek their freedom from suffering in invisible ways that are unexplainable.

This doesn't mean that difficult things won't still occur in your life. It does mean that the impact that those events have on you can be greatly minimized. When we let go of our old pain and suffering, we empower our family and friends to do the same in their own time. Isn't that the most wonderful gift you could give them? All you must do is open your heart and want to heal your pain and the rest happens from there.

Would you rather look at this world as a mess that you are caught up in, or would you like to see it as a miraculous place that you are positively contributing to, just by doing your own inner work? You have that much power, and it needs to be used thoughtfully by understanding the secrets of life and awakening to your purpose. We are all vessels of Love and Light, and we need to reconnect with that Truth for it is the only Truth about us. It is all we have and are. It will never change. It is a Divine gift given to us for all eternity.

# INTUITION

Journal Entry 10/3/16
Lessons versus Purpose with
Archangel Michael and God

**Me:** I have been thinking about my lessons for this lifetime versus just concentrating on my purpose. Are they tied together in some way, Michael?

**Michael:** It is a beautiful contemplation my love. It is also complex. There are many lessons across lifetimes. Each lifetime you have the opportunity to work on them.

**Me:** Okay, so have I been working on specific lessons over many lives? Am I still working on the same ones? What are they?

**Michael:** Yes to both. I am delighted you asked what they are. One is believing in yourself and the other is trusting yourself.

**Me:** This has been difficult for me, but I feel like I am making progress.

**Michael:** You are!

**Me:** I need to continue to trust that I Know what is best for me rather than listening to others. I feel that I will continue to get better with this, and I understand this lesson goes along with this book about intuition. It is interesting that I reach out for help to talk about this and it is you, Michael, that showed up since you dictated this particular book to me.

**Michael:** You are very right. There are no coincidences.

**Me:** God, what can I do to get better at working on this lesson?

**God:** Keep spending time with Me so you are filled up with Knowing who you Truly are and that you can trust your intuition. Your intuition is so strong, and you see it often, yet you deny it at times or question and doubt yourself.

**Me:** I know I do this. I don't honor myself enough to acknowledge the Wisdom I have inside from you.

**God:** We believe in you, Debbie, otherwise you would have not been given these books. We know they are in safe-keeping and that you will bring them out to the world in the most beautiful way.

**Me:** Thank you God. I feel blessed and grateful to be entrusted to spread your words of Love, Hope and Healing.

**God:** Yes. Allow this to keep sinking in. The Love and Wisdom I have shared with you for these books were given to you purposefully as part of your lesson of believing in yourself. If you can't believe in yourself than how will others believe in you? I Know your heart and how much you want to help people, but you need to be confident in your own abilities. When you are not, then the ego thought system kicks in. Do you see this pattern, Debbie?

**Me:** I do see it.

**God:** You forget your strength and abilities. You are a beautiful Light.

**Me:** I am seeing how the victimization patterns and feeling like a fraud are entwined with the lack of belief in myself. This plays out in my life as a belief that I am a failure and this faulty thought sabotages me and decreases my self worth. It dims my Light. This faulty belief then affects my external experience. I manifest what I believe. I need to see these patterns as separate from the wounds I experienced, they are a story I made up.

**God:** Yes, however, the wounds were a story as well. So, you cannot live in that victim world anymore.

**Me:** All my medical issues are attached to those stories as well?

**God:** Yes.

**Me:** I need to stop reliving these stories.

**God:** The story never dies for the wounded or the ego. The ego keeps cultivating fear. It is its own screenwriter of irrational thoughts.

**Me:** Are there other lessons I am working on?

**God:** Yes, but let's just stick with this one for a while until you get stronger with it. It ties into everything else.

### INTUITION

#### Journal Entry 7/16/17
#### with Jesus

**Me:** Jesus, is the urgent pressure I feel to move my career along coming from my ego and will and not the Spirit? Does the Spirit feel any pressure to move forward?

**Jesus:** Interesting question, do you really want to know?

**Me:** Yes! I think it would help me.

**Jesus:** Yes, the Spirit wants to move ahead but understands that there is no such thing as time, so the pressure you feel is actually coming from your ego and your will who want to move forward. They are the source of the urgent pressure you feel. You fear that something won't happen soon enough, or that you are missing out, so you want to move it forward faster.

**Me:** I see, but I also feel excited knowing that I have seen glimpses of the future and I can't wait to live it.

**Jesus:** Your Spirit does not feel urgency, Deb, just Joy.

## BELIEVING IN YOUR SELF

**Me:** So, it is my ego and will?

**Jesus:** Yes, because it doesn't trust that everything will come to you in time. Your Spirit Knows exactly what is coming and does not worry about time.

**Me:** What else do you want to tell me about this?

**Jesus:** Listen to what you heard Joel Osteen say. Be patient and joyful as it all comes together. You need to stay in faith that it will be brought to you.

**Me:** So, I don't need to send out emails or do more radio interviews or advertise?

**Jesus:** It is not necessary, only if you want to. Whether you do it or not does not make any difference to what will come. You see it is not what you do; it has to do with what you were promised, your agreement. Nothing will stop that. Remember, great external achievements do not always come through persons who are Spiritually awake. The journey of someone who is not Spiritually awake can still bring out talents or gifts. But without Spiritual Consciousness the earthly achievements may be great but devoid of what the person needs to accomplish, which is growing their heart and reconnecting with God. Spirit is so much more expansive than what humans can perceive with their senses...and it is through Spirit that God's Light comes to us allowing us to serve others.

**Me:** So, I was thinking about Apple or Microsoft or other tech giants that make amazing technology/products that have spread throughout the world.

**Jesus:** Yes. Many are connected to their creative genius and that is how Earth works, it is self-made. Imagine what someone could do if they were also connected through their heart? Many people are playing a role in society moving it forward in technology and in other ways, but without the understanding of how to connect with people through the heart. That's why many people have more of a relationship with their phone or computer than with the person sitting next to them...or even with themselves.

**Me:** I get it, sort of....

**Jesus:** It will come, it always does. I believe in you, but you must practice believing in yourself.

**Me:** Can you help me know what my Soul Blueprint or Akashic records say, Jesus? What is different about the Soul Blueprint?

# BELIEVING IN YOUR SELF

**Jesus:** It is specific to your Soul growth and gifts and talents you have accumulated.

**Me:** Could you please explain mine?

**Jesus:** No.

**Me:** Why?

**Jesus:** I could, but I don't think it is necessary and it would complicate things for you and distract you on your journey. You have been given insights to some of your past lives, but the rest of it is not in your best interest at this point. Sometimes it creates more interference than good, and we want you to unfold just the way you are. It is perfect and beautiful, and this is what is helping others.

**Me:** If I hadn't gone inside to check with you, I would have sought this information from the outside. That might have led to something that I really don't need to know and didn't think would be harmful in any way. How easy is it to make choices from the urgency of my ego of wanting to know from a place of curiosity rather than what is best for me! Going inside and checking with you, Jesus, is the most important thing I can do with all my choices.

INTUITION

Journal Entry 2/1/18
With John the Baptist

**John:** Debbie, I want to talk with you about all the pressure you put on yourself from believing that you are not enough. I want you to get better with not feeding into this belief.

**Me:** I keep saying something is wrong with me or that I am still broken when there is absolutely nothing wrong with me. I am perfect where I am and as I am. I also struggle because I don't feel the Oneness with everything as I think I should. Why can other people feel the Oneness all the time, John?

**John:** They are lying, Deb. You cannot be in a state of incarnation if that were true.

**Me:** Wow! That takes all the pressure off. The 'I am not enough' belief is so very pervasive in everything I think and do. It is actually fascinating. It is from believing ego thoughts.

**John:** You have a sinus infection again which is just another part of the lessons. This particular illness is all about self-judgment and guilt. You are still trying to control yourself to be better, different, or more expanded by picking on yourself with faulty judgment. All that does is create guilt and shame.

**Me:** I am still judging myself harshly…back to the beginning of Margaret Paul's work. I have not stopped this because I allow ego thoughts to still be in charge. I keep listening to its 'I have to be or should be better or more.'

**John:** *You need to accept yourself as perfect even with the ego voice.* Your resistance to ego thoughts is creating more frustration in you. You need to see it for what it is and let go of the false expectation that it should not be part of your experience. Decide that there is absolutely nothing wrong with you. You are Loved, you are enough, and you are perfect. You need to enjoy being You! It is okay to have goals to shift or correct things that you are working on within yourself, but you need to just let it happen. You cannot force transformation. It is God's job to expand your Consciousness which in turn transforms you.

**Me:** I am still forcing myself forward. I need to let go of these beliefs and unrealistic expectations. I need to know who I AM through God – that He sees me perfect, because I AM.

## Walk with ME in Faith

There will be many times on your path that the belief in separation from Me permeates everything you do and think. It is part of the process of your incarnation. From an awakened state you start to understand the faulty constructs of life that you believe and what follows is a breaking down process of those constructs.

However, the belief in separation continues to linger even as you keep expanding your Consciousness. It is subtle, but it is still very present within your belief system.

Walking with me in Faith – meaning not losing the awareness that there is no separation - helps you to persevere during the times when you still feel separate or alone. As you keep expanding into your natural Divine state, it will become easier to have fewer and fewer moments of feeling separate.

Stay in faith with Me. We are One and never apart. You are a whole Divine being and no faulty construct can ever change that. Step deeper into faith and allow the joy of Oneness to replace every fear of separation. There is only One Heart, One Love, One Consciousness, One You.

-God-

*Life is a miracle.
It allows us to contemplate each moment as an opportunity or as a burden. Each one of us gets to choose each moment of the day how we want to view it. Both views can be found in any situation. It takes an attitude of Love, Forgiveness, Compassion, Mercy, Grace, and Peace to see the beauty in any given situation.
The powers of Love and Grace
are underestimated.*

*I pray that we all have eyes and hearts filled with Grace for ourselves and others.
This will give more meaning to our inner and outer world.*

## INTUITION

We each are born a star, a jewel in our Father's crown that completes it. We are born into this world only to forget who we are, yet we have an urgency to remember something.

Remembering only happens from going within. We spend a lifetime trying to succeed and prove that we are a star that glistens and is special. We forgot that we already are a shining star more brilliant than anyone could imagine; Loved, cherished, and blessed abundantly. We spend lifetimes trying to prove ourselves, being the best, trying to show our worthiness to an illusionary world. If only we remembered that we already are all of this and more, it would stop all the self-imposed stress and angst of delivering ourselves and we could relax and be peaceful. We can then enjoy the miracle of this beautiful life stepping into the amazing Divine destiny that was planned for each one of us. Only then will we come to understand our own perfection, that we already are everything we long to be and that our Father has already delivered us. Finally, we can be One with God and have peace within ourselves and with everyone else.

## Chapter Fourteen

BEING PURPOSELY INTUITIVE

*The more we retain the belief that
we are separate from God and from others
the more we struggle and miss out
on the power and Love of the Universe.*

*I have completed my purpose when I awaken
and accept my Union with God/Divine Love*

Can you imagine living your life through your intuition and the happiness and freedom it would bring? Your intuition is a gift that has been given to you. It is all-seeing and all-Knowing. After all it is God! He will never steer you wrong in any situation and will lead you to your sacred path in life because you are living by Divine design.

Your journey is Divinely orchestrated. Your story has already been written and completed. ***Imagine being fully***

***present and aware that you are co-creating your amazing life with God purposefully!*** God wants to bring you the most spectacular joy filled life you can imagine.

It takes a lot of focus and quiet time to practice the art of hearing and listening to your intuition. Even though your intuition is always there and actively participating in your life, it gets buried under the ego voice. You need to honor your intuition and tune into it, accepting it as the God within you that will never lead you astray. It will always keep you from feeling lost if you allow it.

Your intuition Knows exactly when to change course or what you need emotionally, physically and Spiritually. Over time it will get much easier and you will learn how to stay attuned to it. It becomes your way of life.

When we are attuned to our intuition, we become aware that we share in God's power. We are comfortable with the idea that God has infinite power, but we have a hard time accepting that we (being the same energy) have the same abilities. In fact, we always have that power. That power comes from God's Love, Eternal Life, Peace and Joy, the ability to create through our thoughts and to perceive life as wonderful. We just need to stay present in His peace and open to receive His guidance.

In the three volumes of "A Divinely Ordered Life" book series, I describe how God's Kingdom already resides within you. This is just taking that idea to a deeper level as you strengthen your awareness of the God within.

## BEING PURPOSELY INTUITIVE

You are allowing God's power to guide your life as you become an ever more conscious participant.

This means that you accept all that comes your way rather than being in conflict with life. It does not mean that you love everything coming your way. Many times, you don't care for it at all. Each circumstance is an opportunity, an invitation to see things differently…to shift your perspective, a chance to expand your Consciousness by diving deeper into Love's presence and gift of peace. You are never suffering although many times you perceive that you are. This is an error in thinking. As problems arise during the day, ask God to help you understand what you are feeling, experiencing and how to proceed.

You aren't surrendering. You aren't giving away your power to someone or something outside of your self. You are aligning and getting into agreement with your life force. God's Will is your Will!

Ego will tell you that equating your self with God is narcissistic, but it doesn't understand that you are simply and humbly acknowledging the honor, grace, and privilege that you have been given as Divine creation. You are Divine Consciousness.

We need to embrace our birthright with gratitude and not egotism. We are all One. We all have the same power and abilities. That power is God's Love, Truth and Divine Knowledge.

Imagine looking at your self and everything you

perceive outside of yourself as being the same Light, Spirit, face, or Soul of God appearing in unique, diverse forms. We are One energy; One Consciousness and that Consciousness is Divine Love. We are all Divine beings of goodness, but we struggle to recognize or believe this Truth.

Again, we are a mirror reflection of each other, lost in our forgetfulness and acting as if we know about life. The truth is, that we will never understand life or who we truly are as long as we continue to believe that we are separate from our Creator.

During a meditation this thought came to me that describes the human condition:

> *We are like a flock of sheep grazing in a pasture looking for more grass, not knowing where we are going. God is our shepherd, but if we don't stop wandering in the corners of our mind, we cannot be led to the joy within us. We dwell on our past sufferings and fear of the future. Instead of turning to God to heal and lead us, we continue the suffering within. We continue to destroy our selves passively, again and again emotionally, physically and Spiritually. This is because we do not understand that all things that happen in life are lessons for awakening and to help us*

*remember our Oneness. We forgot that we do not have control over everything, that God is good, and that life is precious. We need to go forward, loving ourselves and others.'*

Our perception of 'the human condition' as being filled with suffering and pain comes from the SPEC and our inability to see our Divinity. Many mistakenly seek God outside themselves. We must seek God from within, and that can be done through our intuition.

We have talked about how we get stuck in the trance of unconsciousness. All of us get caught in this web of misbeliefs and uncertainty. This creates anxiety, depression, addictions, and a host of other issues. To heal from faulty beliefs and experiences and find purpose we need to be present to allow God to help us understand the meaning of each day; otherwise, it is just another day lost. We end up taking the miracle of life for granted.

Staying present is difficult at first. It takes practice and commitment and is something we need to strive for daily. We drift out of the present moment all day long. We get stuck in faulty story lines. Being present is the only way to stay in Divine Truth. This allows you to hear your intuition…God's voice guiding you, validating you and reassuring you.

Being present allows you to connect to your intuition, your inner peace through God. You need to check-in with

## INTUITION

your self several times a day by taking several deep breaths and becoming quiet. Turn your focus inside and forget about the external world for a few moments. This will be helpful in calming yourself from the accumulation of whatever the day or your ego has brought to you.

Once you are calm, ask your self what is best for you to do next and follow through even if it doesn't make sense to you…make sure you're not listening to your ego. Do this several times a day until it becomes a habit. This will help you stay feeling connected to God. Over time, you will start to feel more relaxed and feel that you have more control over your moods, feelings, and behaviors. It is a ***self-regulation*** process that comes from learning you can trust God and yourself more each day. Allow God's grace and Truth to lead your life and you will be happier than you could ever imagine.

Every step of going inward and working on your self is a lifetime worth of work. This is your only real job on Earth, and you can only be engaged in that job when you allow yourself to make time for it. Even as I write these pages, I am aware that at times I AM present listening to my intuition and at other times I am not. This is common because we are all subject to the trance of forgetfulness. We are all caught in the ebb and flow of life, which takes us in and out of Divine Consciousness. Actually, it is a choice to stay present or not. We just forget that it is our choice to make.

## BEING PURPOSELY INTUITIVE

Accepting that the wavering of Consciousness is part of the journey and being compassionate with your self about this process is very important. Do not judge yourself or your progress on the basis of time or earthly achievement.

# Chapter Fifteen

## HAPPINESS IT SHALL BE

*Bringing hope to another human being brings hope to all of humanity through the One collective Consciousness. You accomplish this by claiming your happiness.*

The ultimate goal of your journey is to be happy...happy with yourself, your life, and with the Grace, Love, Protection, Purpose and Eternal life you have been given. When you allow yourself to stay in a state of happiness you are showing gratitude. It is an opportunity to be free from all the pain and misconceptions that you have believed about yourself and others...an opportunity to embrace the Truth of who you truly are and why you are here.

Happiness is an opportunity to serve humanity through your Love and creativity in your own unique way. It is important to remember that serving others is serving yourself because there is only One. Regardless of the way your service unfolds, it will be pure perfection. Just remember that it will unfold according to God's timeline for you, not your own.

There is a life-long transformation occurring within you. It is an expansion of your Consciousness that restructures your programming. It dismantles the false self. The transformation is undoing all the faulty beliefs about yourself and others so you can step into your joyful, magnificent Self.

Over time, True Wisdom will be integrated as the foundation of your belief system. You will develop a Knowingness that is perfect and individualized for your journey.

Just because transformation takes time, it doesn't mean that you are not ready to do what you came here to do right now. You don't have to wait to be transformed to any particular level of Consciousness. As I said before, you are always becoming more of your True nature through the journey.

*Transformation is an expansion in your Consciousness that shifts the way you perceive and understand yourself and life. You learn to perceive through a Divine lens rather than ego programming. It feels very much like a maturing process. I call it being*

## HAPPINESS IT SHALL BE

*"Spiritually re-parented." Over time you will develop a deep trust within. You will Know the source of your intuition is you/God, that God is good and provides the Wisdom for all that you need.*

This doesn't mean that others cannot help you, or that what they have to offer isn't important. Everyone around you is there to teach you something that is very important and necessary to your awakening and evolution of Consciousness. Every experience is purposeful and creates an opportunity to find your way back Home.

Sometimes people are just offering you contrast so you can learn more about yourself by witnessing how you react to something when happy or uncomfortable feelings arise. You become acutely aware of your opinions and beliefs. This teaches you not to judge yourself or others.

Remember, we are all One Consciousness and, as such, it is important to work, support and engage with others. We all have the same Divine purpose. It is to bring Heaven to Earth and share our Creator's Love and Light in our own unique way.

Although each person is an extension of you, (of God) your needs and experiences will be different than those of others. God's Truth never changes, but what is best for you individually will not always be the same as what may be best for others. Everyone is equipped with their own intuition, personal Truth, vision, lessons, path, and purpose for their individual journey. Your intuition will always guide you to that which is True for you and meant for you.

As you begin to feel the exhilaration of the expansion of your Consciousness, you may feel the need to share it with everyone. You feel that everyone would want to know your experience and think, believe, and feel the way you do. It's natural to think that if your path is working for you, then it should work for everyone else as well.

This is simply your loving desire that everyone should share in the awakening, Joy, Peace, and Love that you are beginning to feel. You want to celebrate with your sisters and brothers. The desire is good, but the idea is misplaced. Not everyone is interested in what you have experienced, nor are they ready for what you have to offer. Many people are still asleep and happy to remain so.

You will find other awakened travelers on a similar path as your own and it will be a joy to discuss your mutually shared experiences. Remember that everyone's journey is their own. On the other hand, you may encounter those whose awakened path is completely different than yours with very different beliefs; and that is perfect too.

We simply cannot know what someone else's journey, lessons and purpose is to be. As your awareness grows, you may be able to intuit, a Divine Knowingness, about someone's purpose or path, but this can only be a glimpse or an insight. It isn't a complete understanding. Only your Creator has answers for each individual, since He/you wrote the script.

Let me give you an example. As I have worked with my clients using the tools that I have discussed, I have witnessed clients in session being led by their own Divine guidance in ways that were very different than the ways in which I had been led. I thought my experience was the only correct way. This is the Spiritual ego's limited understanding.

I realized how individualized everyone's guidance truly is. It was and still is a humbling experience for me to confront the pride part of me (something that we all have) that believes it knows everything. I stand in awe when I see how everyone is guided from within on his/her own unique journey. This is how intimately guided each of us is. It is Divine perfection.

It is a blessing to be able to witness the miracle of seeing God's grace and Love guiding, healing, and expanding others to their Highest. It fills me with humility, gratitude, security, and great Love to witness Divine power at work within each of us.

*Become an open invitation for*
*God's Love to transform you.*

# INTUITION

### Journal Entry 4/13/16
### With Archangel Michael

**Michael:** We Love you and you are seeing very well. You see your intuition telling you what is coming next. You just need to keep creating a life of Love. It is the only thing that sticks, that survives. It is the only Truth. We want you to be happy and absolutely love your life.

**Me:** I am happy, but maybe I am not staying in the feeling all day long.

**Michael:** It is okay, just something to remember. *Your happiness shows gratitude.* It is good for you to remember that. We want you to do worship now.

**Me:** What do you mean? How?

**Michael:** By giving grace to everything, yourself included.

**Me:** Is there a particular way?

## HAPPINESS IT SHALL BE

**Michael:** As you pray, keep thinking positive thoughts about you, things, people, and situations. See them through the eyes of Love because ultimately, you are only looking at yourself in everyone else. There is only One Consciousness, so everything is a projection from within you. You need to love all parts of you even the ones that don't understand, can't see, and that are blind to Truth. *They are all you Debbie, your perfect imagination and creation; people in the external world, the faulty beliefs, wounds, and little selves that are crying out for love. They just can't see truth yet.*

**Me:** I will have to work on that.

**Michael:** I don't want you to think this is going to be accomplished quickly. It will take time, but it is a goal I want you to work on. We Love you so much and your awakening is beautiful. Allow me to help you. I hear you asking to stay connected to the Christ Consciousness within, to remove blocks. I want to help you with this, and it will get easier. Just keep calling on me.

**Me:** Who specifically?

**Michael:** All of us, but I am Michael, my wings are holding you tightly as you grow. I want you to feel so Loved and protected. Everything is going according to plan. It will all manifest when it is supposed to.

**Me:** I love that and honor you. You are so beautiful, thank you.

**Michael:** I am you too, Debbie.

*Blessed be the day when life is no longer steeped in the illusion... Where I live from my Highest and see only Love. All that was endured is a faded memory and the glory of who I AM is all that exists.*

You are carried in the palm of God's hand. All you need to do is be open to receiving the blessings that have been bestowed upon you. You are open to receive those blessings when you are tuned in and aligned with the Light within...your intuition. Every day I am reminded that I am Loved and to be happy, that nothing is wrong, all is well! It sounds simple, but it's the work and journey of a lifetime. The goal is to live within God's Truth, safety, and perfection instead of your conditioned programing.

## HAPPINESS IT SHALL BE

To see, feel and Know all of this Wisdom brings true happiness and a great sense of safety, Love, and wholeness within. Everything that we have been searching for on the outside or from others is already waiting within.

Even though we may have gained this important insight, we will continue to waffle back and forth between following the ego or listening to our intuition. It's just the way it is. It will continue to be so until we are finally able to fully integrate and consistently practice and believe our new awareness. There is a difference between intellectually understanding something and believing it to be true. Because we will never fully understand the mystery of life, faith is the only bridge that leads to belief. Ego thoughts will persist; we just gain more mastery of them over time.

What is most important is Knowing that you can always choose to be happy in every moment of every day for it is your True nature. If you should catch yourself being unhappy, it only takes a moment to shift gears. It's all up to you. You make the choice.

## ABOUT THE AUTHOR

Debbie N. Goldberg is a scribe and messenger for God. She is a retired therapist who practiced for eighteen years providing treatment for mental health and substance abuse. She has worked in a variety of settings and is now in private practice as a Divine Therapist and Spiritual Teacher.

She was Spiritually awakened in 2014 by Jesus and taught God's Universal Divine Love and Wisdom. These conversations healed and transformed her life, setting her on a course of self-discovery through Divine introspection with God. Debbie believes that you cannot heal or understand your True identity without the Love and Truth that comes from a one-on-one intimate relationship with God. This ultimately leads you to your Divine calling. Her priority is connecting people to the Divine relationship of Oneness within, as this ends the faulty belief of separation from God that creates pain and suffering.

As part of fulfilling her Divine purpose, she has written two, three-volume book series called 'Creating A Life Worth Living,' first edition, for the Spiritual beginner and

'A Divinely Ordered Life,' second edition, for the more advanced seeker.

Debbie has collaborated and written a chapter in a book called 'Inspired Health Journeys' with nine other seasoned Health Coaches. She has also co-authored two anthologies called Gateway to an Enlightened World - Collective Life Lessons on Personal Transformation and Collective Life Lessons to Support Planetary Transformation. Debbie was a video podcast host on Angel Heart Radio and on Enlightened World Network. She had been involved with programing for Enlightened World Network and participated in several live video broadcasts.

Debbie is helping others understand the journey of Divine self-discovery and Wisdom. She brings the Divine knowledge and experience of her own awakening into her work to inspire healing, love, joy, purpose, and creativity to each of us as we work through our own journey Home.

You can find her book series on Amazon. Debbie credits Jesus, God and the Angels for graciously dictating all of her books and writings.

www.debbiengoldberg.com

## A Divinely Ordered Life on Amazon

https://amzn.to/2IDcf0z

www.facebook.com/groups/681104172576021

www.facebook.com/debbiengoldberg/

www.linkedin.com/in/debbie-goldberg-144a56102/

twitter.com/debbiengoldberg

www.youtube.com/channel/UCO5MMPb0aEpa4TckGl1g2Og

www.pinterest.com/DebbieNGoldberg

www.instagram.com/goldberg.deb/

## ACKNOWLEDGEMENTS

I feel very blessed to be the receiver of this book through Archangel Michael. What a joy it is to know you, Michael, and to know that you are intimately guiding my experience. It is an honor to be the scribe for your beautiful Wisdom.

A huge thank you to my amazing husband who helped me with editing and audio production. Throughout the audio book you will hear intimate conversations between me, God, Jesus, John the Baptist, Archangel Michael, King Solomon, and Archangel Rafael. My husband Brian is the voice for the Divine entities. Brian, your support and love help me bring healing to the world through the Divine gifts that have been given to me. I am so grateful for your patience and service.

My human Angel is Mari-Etta Stoner. I cannot thank you enough for your support, love and time given to edit my book(s). You are sent from Heaven to teach us all what joy and service should look like. I am so appreciative of your friendship.

Thank you, Roy Long of RAL Productions, for your supportive coaching and editing expertise. Without your help Intuition would never have become an audio book.

To God and Jesus, I couldn't have accomplished any of this without your Love, support, and encouragement.

www.ingramcontent.com/pod-product-compliance
Lightning Source LLC
Chambersburg PA
CBHW070537010526
44118CB00012B/1156